Rolling Hills

Book Design & Production:
Columbus Publishing Lab
www.ColumbusPublishingLab.com

Copyright © 2022 by
Charles Hill
LCCN: 2021921391

All rights reserved.
This book, or parts thereof, may not be
reproduced in any form without permission.

Paperback ISBN: 978-1-63337-548-2
E-Book ISBN: 978-1-63337-549-9

Printed in the United States of America
1 3 5 7 9 10 8 6 4 2

―― VIGNETTES *of a* LIFE *in* OHIO ――
Rolling Hills

Charles W. Hill

*This book is dedicated to my parents,
Austin R. Hill and Bessie Maude Nutter Hill.
They were excellent parents to their four sons.*

*Dedicated also to their two sons,
my brothers, who died far too soon:*

*Pvt. Robert Warren
Fremonville, France,
11–19–44*

*Richard Lewis in a truck accident
near Newport, Ohio,
7–13–45*

CONTENTS

INTRODUCTION I

PART ONE: BEGINNINGS III
CHAPTER 1   THE HOUSE 1

PART TWO: BEYOND THE HOUSE 33
CHAPTER 2   THE ORCHARD 35
CHAPTER 3   THE BARN 37
CHAPTER 4   MY HUNDRED ACRES
                OF ADVENTURE SPACE 47
CHAPTER 5   PLANTING SEASON 57

PART THREE: THE LARGER COMMUNITY 71
CHAPTER 6   THE M.E. CHURCH 73
CHAPTER 7   THE PALMER
                ELEMENTARY SCHOOL 89
CHAPTER 8   MEMBERS OF THE
                NEIGHBORHOOD 101
CHAPTER 9   THE CENTERS
                OF SHOPPING 115
CHAPTER 10   LIFE CHANGED FOREVER 125
CHAPTER 11   A SECOND SEARCH 147
CHAPTER 12   A NEW SCHOOL 151
CHAPTER 13   A NEW CHURCH 163
CHAPTER 14   THE SECOND FARM AND
                MY TEENAGE YEARS 173
CHAPTER 15   THE DECISION OF
                A LIFETIME 195
CHAPTER 16   REFLECTIONS 205

INTRODUCTION

EVERY LIFE HAS A STORY to tell. Most never get shared for a number of reasons. I suppose that some think their experience of life is so common that it isn't worth sharing. Others may be so busy that they never get around to setting pen to paper.

In many ways my life has been quite normal. Yes, as I look back across more than eighty years, I clearly see some moments that I want to share with my children, grandchildren, great-grandchildren, and anyone else who may want a short glimpse into farm life as it was lived in the rolling hills of southeastern Ohio in the 1930s and 1940s.

Life for me began in the front bedroom in an old, nine-room farmhouse that stood for more than a century on a one-hundred-acre farm along a township road in Palmer Township, Washington County, Ohio. The attending physician was W. D. Turner, whose office was in Beverly, Ohio, seven miles away. I remember life in that setting better than any place I have ever lived. First impressions do leave a major mark on the memory screens of most lives.

On December 5, 1944, my family received word that my oldest brother, Robert Warren, had been killed in France. His death occurred on

November 19 during battle in a place named Fremonville. Robert was a replacement for deceased and seriously wounded soldiers. He was in battle less than thirty days. As a result of that death, my father suffered grief, immediately put the farm up for sale, and moved our family to Waterford, a small town about seven miles away. He moved in an attempt to assuage his grief. But less than three months after making that move, my brother Richard Lewis was killed in a truck accident. We would soon move again.

This time we relocated to a new farm about six miles from the first. That move was made in October 1946. It was the place where I moved from adolescence toward young adulthood. I was graduated from high school, fell in love, and married Betty L. Maze, who was a beautiful young woman.

After marriage, Betty and I first lived in a small, eighteen-foot trailer, and later in a forty-foot mobile home. In the spring of 1955, we moved our mobile home to Pike County, where I had been employed by the Goodyear Atomic Corporation since December the previous year. Anita and Barbara were both born in those early years.

It was at the Beaver Methodist Church (now United Methodist) on an October Sunday evening in 1955 that I responded positively to the call to follow Christ. As I knelt at the chancel rail, Betty joined me, and a new life focus soon became clear. For the next fifty years we would serve Christ as we led Methodist and then United Methodist Churches in several places across the West Ohio Conference of the denomination.

During the early years of ministry, we were blessed with two more daughters: Elizabeth, born while we were serving Rodney Charge and I was attending Rio Grande College, now the University of Rio Grande. Bethany, our fourth and final child was born while we were serving Derby Circuit, and I was attending the Methodist Theological School in Ohio, at Delaware.

PART ONE
BEGINNINGS

CHAPTER 1

THE HOUSE

THE OLD FARMHOUSE where I was born in the early morning hours of Wednesday, September 27, 1933, at 12:30 a.m., stood firm for 130 years until the summer of 2019, when it was razed to make way for a new, smaller, modern structure. The old house, which I knew so well, continues to be quite visible on the memory screen of my still-viable mind. In the following pages, I will share some of that structure's uniqueness. It was more than a place just to live and grow. It was where I first learned what it means to be part of a family, part of a family that works together, cares for each other, and knows what it is to be a responsible human being. I may not have always followed what I knew was right, but I did not flout those early teachings with impunity.

The two-story, nine-room house stood just off a township road on the east side of Palmer Square. The Square was about a mile wide on all sides. There were about a dozen farmhouses around that special block of land. Our house contained porches in front and back. Attached to the back porch was an addition containing a wash house and woodshed. The porch, wash house, and woodshed were added after Dad and Mom bought the place in 1929. My grandfather, Jacob Hill, possessed carpenter skills, so he was the overseer of that work. The front porch was for relaxing, and the back porch was used for many purposes.

The old house was surrounded by several large maple trees that were wonderful gifts through which the summer evening breezes cooled the air. This made the upstairs bedroom more comfortable as my brothers Bob, Bill, Dick, and I slept. Yes, all four of us slept in the same room, two to a bed. One memory of that bedroom, unrelated to sleeping, comes to mind.

One year Aunt Hattie and Bruce, our cousin who lived in Grandville, Michigan, were with us at Eastertime. Mother, Aunt Hattie, and we kids had colored some of our farm eggs for the occasion. Sometime over that weekend it was decided we should have an Easter egg hunt. So, the boiled eggs were hidden in various rooms of the house, and the rest of us hunted for them. I don't know that there was a count taken before the fun began, but there was a lot of noise and laughter. After the hunt ended, we ate the eggs. Later, maybe toward the end of summer, Mother was looking through clothing hanging in our bedroom closet. She was probably checking out our clothing for school. As Mom went about that work, she was quite surprised to find eggs, aged eggs, spoiled eggs, still in pockets where someone had put them at Easter. They were handled very gingerly and ushered out, probably to the bucket of stuff that was fed to the hogs. The proper name for that stuff was slop.

The interior of that old house still lives vividly in my mind. I can, after all these years (we moved away in April of 1945), mentally move through every aspect of the place, seeing sights I haven't physically experienced for more than seventy-five years. The house consisted of a cellar, first floor, upstairs, and attic. The attic was one place where we boys, usually Dick and I, could go sometimes on rainy days and goof off. There was a huge map of Barlow Township spread out on the floor there. Dick and I often perused it, but that was a long time ago. All I can really remember now is that the map was very large and color-coded. The Waterman Family (whose ancestors were among some of the first settlers in this part of Washington County) from whom the farm was purchased, told Mom and Dad that the attic was one of the areas where drillers, tool dressers, and roustabouts slept when the great southern Ohio oil boom was on. Those days were in the late nineteenth and early twentieth centuries. And it must have been a real boom time. One man in Waterford, whose parents had struck oil near the Muskingum River, is reported to have said, "Money was coming in so fast we didn't know what to do with it." Wouldn't that be a nice problem? Well, back to the attic.

The steps leading up to that attic were sometimes used by my brothers as a back-drop for telling ghost stories. Some of the words spoken were, "I'm coming to get you. I'm on the first step. I'm on the second step," etc. At some point the voice would yell, "Got you!" At that very moment, the "ghost" would grab someone. No matter how hard we tried, when the voice said, "Got you," and someone grabbed us, we jumped and yelled.

The second floor of the house contained four bedrooms and a large hallway. One room was where we four boys slept. Another was where, for many years, my Aunt Hattie's furniture was stored. It was placed there when she and my uncle Roland Ormiston (Hoolie) moved to Michigan in the late 1930s. There they bought a mobile home. Later, they purchased a house, but didn't come for the furniture. Most of that stuff was not removed until April 1945, when we had our farm sale. The other two bedrooms were kept ready for any guests who might come to visit for a day or two.

Not many people came to stay overnight. In addition to Aunt Hattie's annual visits, I recall that Aunt Grace, one of Mother's many sisters, and three of her daughters, came once for a week's visit. That was a fun time for me. I am not certain Mother fully enjoyed the extra cooking and such. Cousin Georgia and I seemed to hit it off quite well. She was a bit older than I. The last time I visited with her, just a few years ago in Richmond, Ohio, she was still reminding me about how I plugged several watermelons looking for a ripe one. I turned the green ones over so the plug would not show. Of course, those melons rotted, and later, when Dad discovered my sin, he was not at all pleased. Cousin Georgia died a few years ago. She was a really lovely person.

It was in that bedroom, the one where Aunt Grace and her daughters slept, we discovered (after the fact) that house and family had escaped a catastrophe one winter night.

It was a very cold night. Bill and I were the only ones at home. I have no idea now where the rest of the family had gone. There was a robust fire in the dining room circulating heater when we noticed an odor that indicated something might be burning. We were momentarily frightened. We quickly checked the house upstairs and down but saw no fire. In a short while the odor vanished, and we thought nothing more about it.

Sometime, weeks or months later, during daylight hours, Mom entered that upstairs bedroom and discovered that the wallpaper covering an opening in the chimney had burned off. There was supposed to be a metal disc inserted securely into the chimney to prevent fire and smoke from escaping into the room. Someone, however, had taken a shortcut when papering the room. They ignored all safety rules and just papered over the opening in the chimney. (Someone may have planned to remove the paper later and install the metal cover but forgot to do it.) The roaring fire on that cold night heated the wallpaper until it ignited and burned off the opening. We were so fortunate that it burned only the paper covering. The residue was probably sucked up the chimney, thereby preventing embers from falling onto the rug or bed and starting a conflagration. Sometimes close calls are simply that—close calls. Sometimes they cause real destruction. The Hill family was truly fortunate that night. A fire in the countryside during those days meant the house and its contents were a total loss.

Also, on that second floor was a major hallway. A hefty wooden table stood in that hallway. A length of stove pipe was wrapped around each of the table legs. The table was used for storing flour. In the late summer after the wheat harvest, Dad would take several bushels of new wheat down to the Lowell Mill to exchange for sacks of flour. The flour was then stored on the table. The stove pipe sections were used to keep mice from getting at that wonderful substance with which Mother made the tastiest bread and pastries.

Before we leave the upstairs, it is important to state that there was no heat up there in winter. When it was ten degrees outside, we slept under lots of covers.

Mother purchased for our bed special flannel sheets. These sheets were double length, so when they were properly folded, we slept on one part of the sheet and were covered by the other part. With the addition of a couple of quilts, we kept fairly warm. For years there had been talk of cutting a hole in the floor, inserting a register, and allowing heat from the kitchen to rise up to our bedroom. Just a few years before we moved away, that dream was made a reality. Wow! It certainly made a lot of difference in the comfort of that bedroom in winter. Dad was always a bit slow, it seems to me, in making progressive improvements, no matter how big or small.

As I wrote the last line above, I was reminded of a conversation Chester Moody had with Dr. Hill (not related to me), our local physician. Chester ran a garage at Barlow, about five miles from Palmer. The good doctor had a vintage Ford car. Chester was looking it over one day while Doc was at Chester's Barlow place of business. As Chester checked out the doctor's car, he noticed that the tires were slick. As Moody put it, "As slick as a spanked baby's behind." The tread was all gone. Chester told the doctor that he needed new tires, and he would put a new set on for him. Chester reported, "Doc walked around the car and carefully felt of the tires, pondered the issue for a short time, and then looked at me and said, 'Mr. Moody, I believe they'll be OK for another year.'" That was probably true, for the good doctor never drove over thirty- or thirty-five miles an hour. The good Doc too, was slow to make changes.

Dr. Hill was frugal. A story, without question, apocryphal, made its rounds throughout the Vincent Community. It stated that Doc went to

Tommy Roberts' Store in Vincent and purchased two eggs—one for himself and one for his wife, Lucy. It was near dinner time. Later that night, so the story goes, Doc returned to the store with one of the eggs. "Lucy didn't want her egg," he told the store owner. Doc wanted a refund.

The kitchen of our house was, of course, on the first floor. It was the room where we gathered around a drop leaf table for breakfast most every morning. The cook stove was a Kalamazoo wood and coal range. It was cream and green colored, and had compartments on the back where food could be kept warm. Also, there was a reservoir on one end of the unit. It kept water warm, sort of. Of course, every morning a fire had to be started in that stove before any cooking could begin. It took time to get the kindling started and then for the wood and coal to ignite. But gradually it happened, and Mother would put breakfast on the table. That stove provided a lot of good food for our family when Mother was at the helm.

One hilarious moment comes to mind as I remember that stove. In the early spring we often tapped maple trees and made syrup from the sap. One day, Dad was about to take a bath and found a pan of "water" boiling on the stove. He took some of it for his bath. But as he engaged in the bathing process, he began to feel sticky. At first he didn't quite understand what the problem was. Then it suddenly hit him. He was bathing in hot maple sap. He had to take a second bath. Even many years later, the whole family would laugh about Dad's sugary mistake.

One morning my older brothers, Bob and Bill, engaged in a pancake eating contest. They each ate several, maybe as many as nine or ten. I think Bill won, but I am sure both were at least a bit sick when it was over. The pancakes were large. I don't remember that they ever again engaged in such a competition. I do remember a lot of laughter as Mother kept the cakes coming to the table. A good memory.

Also, one evening we were eating supper at that table when we heard our neighbor, Peck (Raymond Reed), a man who possessed a large vocabulary of words we boys were not allowed to use, yelling at his horses. From our places at the table, we could see and hear him screaming at the work animals, yet they were not moving an inch. We had noticed for some time that one of the horses breathed very loudly. We could hear that animal breathing when it was at a major distance. This was probably caused by recurrent airway obstruction, also known as "broken wind." Neighbor Peck kept on working the animal just the same. He used a whip from time to time as well. As he was yelling and cursing at his team, the broken wind horse suddenly dropped to the ground like a ton of bricks. At that moment, supper was over.

We boys raced over to the spot where the horse had fallen. That beautiful animal was dead. I thought our neighbor would be distraught and show some compassion. But by the time we arrived on the scene, he was pulling the harness from the dead animal and saying, "Guess I'll have to break in another one." That was about it. No emotion. No compassion, and, seemingly, no regret that he had screamed and yelled at the poor dying animal that had served him well for many years. At least that is the way it seemed to me. I was stunned.

That scene still haunts me from time to time. We were taught to be as kind as possible to our animals, and not to abuse any of God's creatures. Of course, it is hard to be compassionate when cutting off a chicken's head or shooting animals for food. But we can be respectful by not wasting any of that food for which the animal has given its life.

As I remembered the event mentioned above, I was reminded of a very large elm tree that stood near where the horse had fallen. Branches of that huge tree hung out over the township road. If one were walking along that path after night, it was spooky. It could cause a bit of fear in a boy, make hair on the back of his neck stand up, encourage him to step up his pace. Sometimes it was more than the tree that could cause one's hair to stand on end. Part of the time this tree was the home of a very loud screech owl. When that bird sounded out his bloodcurdling shriek, one wanted to run—fast. In fact, many a night we could hear the owl's mournful wailing, even after we had gone to bed. Of course, in summer the windows were always open to let the night air cool the room where we slept, therefore outside noises were quite pronounced. The sound of whippoorwills—that familiar, "Whip-poor-will," over and over—was also one of the summer evening sounds that carried us off to dreamland. There is no other serenade of nature quite as soothing to the soul as, "Whip-poor-will."

On the east wall of the kitchen stood a sink and pitcher pump. There was no running water in the house except when someone moved the pump handle up and down. The sink was mostly for washing hands. Also, Dad used it for shaving. I can still see him standing before a mirror that hung above the sink, sharpening his straight razor, using a leather strop that was attached to a wall hook nearby. He would sharpen it a bit, then see how easily it removed hair from his forearm. He might sharpen it some more. When satisfied with its readiness, he would take a shaving brush, dampen it, place the bristle end in the cup that contained a cake of special soap, and create foam, which he then brushed on his face. Next, he would take that straight razor and slide it down his face, removing his whiskers. As a kid, I was always astonished that he didn't cut himself. He may have nicked his face a few times, but never anything serious. The process looked very dangerous to me. The time or two when I decided to inspect that tool more closely, I ended up with a bleeding thumb.

Dish washing was not done in the kitchen sink, but in a large pan on the stove. Once washed, dishes were transferred to a second pan that contained rinse water. Last of all, the dishes were towel dried by one of us boys. Attached to the wall above the sink, was an oil lamp with a moveable mirror behind it. In winter, when darkness came early, we could, with that mirror, focus the lamp's light beam on the dish pan to help us see if the dishes were washed clean. Truth of the matter is, that beam of light was a poor substitute for the real thing. It was more like a flashlight with dying batteries or a campfire slowly fading away. How fortunate most of us are today. We have electricity. It is everywhere. We put our dishes into a machine, add detergent, close the door, turn the knob; and in a little while, the dishes are clean, and we have read a chapter or two in a good book.

In summer, the heat of that stove made the task of dish washing even more uncomfortable. The work was boring, and it made the laborers more uncomfortable. Wash and dry and sweat. Often on Sunday, Dad would say to one of us boys, "Come and help me with the dishes." He felt that Mother should be given a short vacation from that work on the Lord's Day. And it also demonstrated to us boys that we too could help with household duties.

Some years ago, while serving as pastor to a large suburban congregation I, along with some other adult assistants, took a group of junior high youth on a weekend retreat. We agreed that to keep costs low, we would do our own cooking. Cleanup would be done by teams of youth assigned to the task. Each assigned cleanup group did a stellar job. One problem did occur on the last day. On Sunday, about noon, we shared a final meal and began preparing to leave. Of course, the dishes had to be washed. The assigned team began the process, and all was progressing as planned. One father, however, came a little early to pick up his daughter. As he approached the door, he asked where he could find his daughter. Someone told him she was inside helping with cleanup. He came into the large gathering area, saw his daughter with her hands in the dish pan, and asked in a rather condescending tone, "What are you doing?" She replied that it was her turn to help with cleanup. "Get your hands out of that water," he demanded. "You don't do that at home, and you are not going to do it here." I wondered if the man knew anything about parenting. I am sure his daughter was embarrassed. Some parents just do not understand the basics.

Against the north wall of the kitchen sat the wood box. It had to be filled every day or two so Mom would have fuel for cooking. My first, assigned daily task was to see that the box had wood in it. One evening, Mom and I were sitting in the dining room, where the family usually gathered at end of day during fall and winter. It was already dark outside. Dad came in from somewhere, probably the barn, and for some reason looked in the wood box. He came into the room where we were sitting and announced that the box was empty. He then turned and left. I thought he was going to the woodshed. Instead, he returned with a lighted lantern. "Come on," he said, "I will hold the light for you." So out to the woodshed we went. As I recall, we made two or three trips, with me carrying a few sticks of wood each time. Then Dad pitched in and carried as much in one trip as I could in several. He never yelled. He did not scold. But he did teach me a wonderful lesson: If you have been assigned a task to do, then do it.

At our house, when there was work to be done, and there always was, we all were expected to be involved. Washing dishes, sweeping floors, taking slop to the hogs, or filling the wood box was not a disgrace. Work was good, and it was necessary that each of us pull his weight.

Just above the wood box was the telephone. The first phone had been in the parlor, but lightning had hit that side of the house during a summer thunderstorm and ripped it off the wall. When the phone was replaced, it was moved to the kitchen where it was more convenient for those who would answer the call. On occasion the phone was a window to our very limited world. Our phone line was a party line. That means that we were on the same system as four or five other families. Each family had an assigned ring. Maybe a long and two shorts. Another might have a long and three shorts. These rings were achieved by turning a crank on the side of the wooden phone box. If one were careful, the receiver could be lifted, and we could listen in on any conversation our neighbors were having. On occasion someone might say, "I think someone is listening to us." Then the eavesdropper would be a bit embarrassed, maybe, but probably not hang up.

One Sunday afternoon our parents were away, and an older boy from the community was visiting. His great aunt lived with him, his mother,

THE HOUSE

and his grandparents, just a few miles away. He knew his great aunt was alone that afternoon and his mother and grandparents were away. He called home, knowing his aged aunt would answer the phone. She answered. He did not identify himself but moved right ahead with his plan. He inquired, "Does the state highway run past your house?" She said it did. He then continued, "If it isn't too much trouble, would you please run out and catch it for me?" He then quickly hung up. I hope she thought it was funny too. All of us boys did.

Later that boy was inducted into the army. When he came home on furlough from boot camp, Mom, Dad, and I went to visit him, his mother, and grandparents. He had an impressive string of medals hanging down the front of his jacket. Dad asked about them. He knew that the young man had just come from boot camp, and that to have earned all those honorary medals would certainly have taken longer than a few weeks. "Oh," the young soldier responded, "I bought them at the PX." There is certainly more than one way to gain prestige and feed the ego.

Along the kitchen's east wall stood an old-fashioned cabinet where flour, sugar, and other items used in cooking were stored. This cabinet contained a metal work surface that could be pulled out when needed. Mother kneaded bread dough, rolled out pie crusts, noodles, and other delicacies on that workspace. And I used that surface to prepare from scratch my first cakes. Being the youngest of four boys had its positives and negatives. The youngest usually had it a bit easier. But this was farm life. There were no girls in our family. Being the youngest boy, I was expected to do double duty: work in the field and help in the house.

Dad could look up at the sun, tell when it was almost lunch time and say, "Time for you to run in and help Mom get food on the table." Following lunch, I would have to stay and help with cleanup, that means wash dishes, and then go to the field. I thought double duty was a bit much. Yet, during those early years I learned some things about cooking that have been quite helpful across the years. And they are especially helpful now that I do all the cooking. My wife, Betty, has some neurological issues that prevent her from engaging in that art. She did it very well across the years for our daughters and me. Now it falls to the Old Man to return the favor. And I am grateful that I can. Of course, I don't do it as well as she did it, but with some instruction from her, we get by.

It was in that kitchen one night when I was about ten years old, having enough knowledge to read recipes, I decided to make some chocolate candy. I had the cocoa and sugar mixed when Mother entered the room. She scolded me a bit, saying I was using up the whole ration of sugar (many things were rationed during World War II), and we would be short. Then she helped me complete the job. That night I learned a truth: Sometimes it is better to ask before acting. Yet, I am also aware that sometimes it is just as easy to go ahead and do what one wants and then take the heat for it. A little heat for a few pieces of fudge was not a bad trade off.

Another memorable event took place in that kitchen. Mother used to make a cereal that was called Homemade Grape Nuts. She mixed the batter and baked it in the oven. When done and cooled, the product was quite hard. It was then broken into small pieces and processed through a food chopper. On this particular day, it was Bill who was turning the chopper handle. For some reason, when there was a break in the turning of the handle, Dick pushed a finger into one of the openings where the product came out. Just as he did that, Bill gave the handle a turn. Dick lost some skin and a bit of flesh from his finger. As I remembered it, Dad and Mom took Dick to Dr. Turner in Beverly to have it dressed. But my brother informed me that they talked about it and decided they could take care of it themselves. And they did.

We were not rushed to the doctor on a whim in those days. The wound had to be major. I know, because I was carrying a double-bitted axe on my shoulder one evening, stumbled a little, and the axe bounced up and cut the back of my head. I went weeping to the house with blood on my hands. Dad washed the area, clipped the hair off around the wound, put iodine on the cut, and bandaged it. In a few days I was good as new. No doctors needed.

On another occasion, it was Bill who needed a doctor. He had been sick for a few days. He had scarlet fever. He was confined to bed. One afternoon he began to hallucinate. He saw calves running in places where there were none. Dad called Dr. Turner, who kept an office in Beverly. The good doctor, the family physician who had delivered me, came about mid-afternoon. He examined my brother, who had a high fever. The doctor probably gave Bill something for the fever. Then the doctor told Mom and Dad he was going to give Bill a medicine he had never used before. It was something new. It was called sulfa. It was reported to be very effective at killing infection.

The next day, Dr. Turner came back out the seven miles to check on Bill. No one had called him. He was just very concerned. He had told a neighbor whom he had also seen that afternoon that he wasn't sure the Hill boy would live. When the doctor returned, he found Bill had made some improvement. The problem was that as his body fought off scarlet fever, he had developed Bright's disease, which is a major inflammation of the kidneys. Bright's disease was, before 1900, considered incurable. Teddy Roosevelt's first wife died of it, as did Emily Dickinson, Chester A. Arthur, and many others. Some time ago Bill was told that his bout with Bright's disease probably caused his heart arrhythmia problem. He has taken medication across many years for that malady.

Just off the kitchen was the pantry. Many items were stored in that small room. It was also where the cream separator was kept. This machine separated cream from milk. It was operated manually by turning a handle. As the handle was turned, some special discs rotated at a very high rate of speed. As the whole milk moved down through those discs, the milk and cream were separated. Cream came out one spout and Blue John the other. Sometimes, just to be doing something, I would go into the pantry and rev up the cream separator and make it sing. I could really make it go, until Mother would yell, "That's enough." And when Mother spoke, we all listened intensely. Usually.

In these early years we sold cream to Paul Huck at Waterford. Later, when the United Dairy came to Waterford, we milked cows and sold grade B milk. Without electricity, there was no refrigeration. Dad dug a rectangular hole in the ground, cemented it on all sides and in the bottom, filled it with two feet or so of water, and then the ten-gallon cans were placed there each evening for cooling. The milkman would retrieve them the next morning when he came. It worked well to keep the milk from going bad. Also, sometime in the early 1940s, Dad purchased a Chore Boy milking machine. It was powered by a gasoline engine. That purchase greatly speeded up the milking process. But it still took quite a lot of time to clean the equipment when milking was completed. Sometimes it seems when one task is made easier, another demand suddenly appears.

Adjoining the kitchen was a dining room that contained a large oval table, circulating wood and coal heating stove, icebox, later a refrigerator, and the radio. There were many joyous meals held around that table. Of course, when neighbors came to help with thrashing and silo filling, the table would have to be extended to its optimum length. There was always a lot of laughter and conversation at that time. One day, during one of these meals, Mr. Carl Strauss, who was helping with the work, told my Aunt Helen, who was assisting Mother with the meal, that they missed him with the pie. Mr. Strauss told Aunt Helen he didn't get any. Mom told Aunt Helen that she knew he had received a piece of pie like all the rest, but Mr. Strauss insisted. So Mom told my aunt to give him a quarter of a pumpkin pie. She did. He finished it off, then pulled the original piece of pie from under the table and ate it. Mr. Strauss was quite a cutup. He was a really good man as well.

One day when I was quite young, Mother told me I could go in and clear the crumbs off the table after our noon meal. I grabbed the dishcloth and hurried into the dining room. I slowly gathered some crumbs to the side and then brushed them onto the floor. I don't know how many times I repeated that act before Mother saw the way I was clearing the table of crumbs. "Oh!" she shouted in an alarming tone. "Don't put them on the floor. Gather them in your hand and put them in the sink." Oft-times in life it has taken two or three attempts for me to get things right. But I always try to remember not to put the crumbs on the floor. I had part of it right. I used the dishcloth.

It was also around that table that we shared a special dinner in August of 1944. We didn't know at the time that it would be our last meal as a complete family. Brother Bob had been home on a delay in route. He was in the army. His basic training had been at Fort Walters, Texas. Now the time had come for him to go overseas. His young wife of three or four days, Eileen Henderson, was at the table also. Mother had prepared well, but there was a depressing cloud of pain and uncertainty that totally encompassed us. I remember that Dad did not eat much. He didn't go to the train station with the others. Bill, Mom, and Eileen accompanied Bob to Parkersburg, West Virginia, where he boarded the train that transported him and other soldiers to Fort Meade, Maryland. From there Bob shipped overseas. He was killed on November 19, 1944. We did not receive the telegram until December 5th. My family and Eileen's family shared Christmas dinner that year at her parents' home in Beverly, Ohio. We were all sad together. Pain that is shared is sometimes easier to bear.

Recently as I was visiting the Oliver Tucker Museum in Beverly, I suddenly realized that just below me was the house in which the Henderson family had lived. After all these years, that Christmas dinner hit my memory screen like a flash fire. Some experiences just never fully leave us.

While Bob was home on that delay in route, it was thrashing season. One day Dad had gone to a neighboring farm to help with that annual task. I remember Mother telling him to "stay off the stack." The man on the stack was responsible for shaping that mound of straw so it would be balanced and firm. He stood under or near the blower that transported the straw from the separator. Sometimes the straw fell right on the stacker's head. That is why Mother told Dad to stay off it. Dad probably laughed and waved goodbye. He often volunteered for the worst job, the one nobody else wanted.

Later in the morning I rode my bike up to that neighbor's place. The man of the farm met me in the yard. He was really upset that Bob had not come up to help. The man was livid. I didn't remain there long. Bob had stayed with Mother. It was wash day. He had decided to stay and help her. I am glad he did. Certainly, Mother long remembered that day as special when she and her oldest son enjoyed some real quality time together. Just the two of them. The last time.

In the summer of 2018, Bethany, our youngest daughter, who, during her college years was fortunate enough to spend some time studying in France, visited the rural town of Fremonville where Bob was killed. She and a college friend were treated like royalty there. It was, for her, a very moving experience. She told me recently that the community of Fremonville, France, had celebrated, in a major way, the seventy-fifth anniversary of their liberation by the Allied Forces. They were still very grateful for all that the American soldiers had done for them back in the day when Hitler had been stopped from ruling the world.

Brother Robert Warren Hill was assigned to F Company, Second Battalion, 314th Regiment, Seventy-ninth Infantry Division. It has been determined that he had been in battle for several days then pulled back for rest. His last letter was written on November 10, 1944, which was the eve of his return to the battlefront with fellow soldiers. He was killed nine days later. The two Second World War buffs who talked with Bethany Hill Anderson and her friend Elizabeth explained that Bob was buried in a cemetery in Epinal, France, along with other American soldiers. His body remained there until 1947 when it was exhumed and returned to the United States at his family's request. His remains now rest in the cemetery at Beverly, Ohio. The story of Bethany's visit was featured in the Luneville, France, newspaper.

Now back to the house. On one wall of the dining room, there was a large piece of slate that Dad installed. I think it came from an old schoolhouse that was no longer in use. On that blackboard we boys worked out math problems and practiced our spelling words. Most evenings there was a lot of activity around that piece of slate. It probably helped us much more than television or cell phones would have. Of course, those devices had not yet become available. When Mom and Dad were away, that blackboard was sometimes used to display images that would be funny only to a group of unruly farm boys. The artwork was usually gone by the time Mom and Dad returned, and that was a good thing.

As stated earlier, there was no electricity in the house. So when we went from room to room at night, an oil lamp had to be carried to illuminate the way. One needed to be very careful when carrying the light, for a dropped lamp could start a fire that would burn the house down. We used oil lamps on a regular basis, but when we wanted extra light, Mom would fire up our Aladdin Lamp. It used white gas under pressure. Put the gasoline in, pump up a bit of pressure, then light the lamp. The mantel would glow brightly and light up the whole room. One night I put my hand above the lamp chimney and noted that there was a lot of heat there. So I found some marshmallows, put one on a fork, and held it over the chimney to roast it. Everything was going just fine until the marshmallow became soft and fell off the fork and hit the mantel. That very delicate part of the lamp totally disintegrated. The light went out, and then Mother made me feel another kind of heat. Oh, just the heat of words, nothing physical.

Of course, because of the lack of electricity, there were neither running water nor bathroom facilities. There was an outhouse that, after the mid-nineteen thirties, was referred to as The Roosevelt. That was because the construction of these units was a part of President Franklin Roosevelt's work projects, which provided jobs for men who were frantic for employment and a little income so they could feed their families. These toilets replaced the old two- or three-seaters and also improved sanitation (I think) for rural families. Some folks, even my parents, made fun of the President's work programs. But those employment opportunities helped to feed a lot of families. They also assisted the nation in its move toward economic recovery. Strange how political beliefs can cause people to vote against themselves. It happens even now.

I mentioned a refrigerator earlier. We did get one of those about 1940. It was used and operated on kerosene. What a welcome addition it was to our house. Before that we used an icebox. Every few days in summer, a delivery truck from Beverly Ice would come through the community, stopping at each house that might want a small block or two. We most always purchased some blocks. I think in those days a good-sized chunk of ice cost twenty-five cents, maybe less. The problem with the icebox was that the pan underneath, which caught the melt water, had to be emptied regularly. If it was not emptied on time, water would run across the floor. And when that happened, someone would be charged with dereliction of duty. We did not often forget to empty that pan.

I should also say here that Uncle Ernest, Dad's youngest brother, brought the refrigerator in his pickup truck from West Virginia to the farm. I think he had talked with Mom and Dad, made the deal, then delivered the appliance. He also worked to get it functioning, then showed us how to keep it operating. As I recall, there were no problems unless someone forgot to refill the tank that held the kerosene. When that unwelcome situation occurred, it was made known quickly by harsh fumes yelling, "The flame is out, *DO* something." The refrigerator made a major difference in the way we handled perishable food. It was a wonderful addition to our move toward better living.

The dining room was also the place where the Saturday night baths for us boys took place in cold weather, because the heating stove was in that room. As the youngest, I was usually first into the bath. Then the others followed. Yes, same water. I guess it could be said that we bathed in series and in public. Summer was different. The number nine wash tub was moved outside or placed on the back porch for that weekly ritual. Looking back, I still see clear images of one or two of those public baths.

There are certain sounds and smells from that old house that still bless my life. Often in winter I was awakened by a sound that my children or grandchildren never heard. It was the sound of Dad shaking down the ashes and breaking up clinkers in the heating stove. Sometimes it seemed that the whole house shook. He would bank the fire at night by adding coal and closing off most of the draft, or air flow. This caused the coal to burn very slowly and form a hard crust on top. To get the fire going in the morning, you had to break up that crust. After some poking and shaking, the coal would blaze up, heat the stove, and the stove would heat the house. At least some small part of it.

Most every morning after the clinkers were shaken down and the house began to warm, there would be noise in the kitchen. Those clanking sounds were often followed by the aroma of eggs and bacon frying. That would mean it was seven o'clock. At seven we would hear the voice of Mrs. E. Howard Cadel coming through our radio singing, "Ere you left your room this morning, did you think to pray?" That song meant we were to get up and get going, and hopefully ask God's blessing on our day.

During World War II everything was rationed. It was impossible to get many items that were necessary to maintain our living experience the way we had when the nation was at peace. So we resorted to human ingenuity. One necessary item was presentable floor covering, especially linoleum. Our kitchen linoleum was looking really exhausted. New linoleum could not be purchased, so we painted the old covering solid gray. Then we took small pieces of sponge and created designs on the gray background—designs in red, yellow, and white. It looked great, for a while.

ROLLING HILLS

Sugar was rationed in those days too. At some point during the war, Bill was able to purchase ten pounds of that sweet stuff on the black market. I am not sure, but I think it was obtained through a village official in Beverly. I suppose my parents expected to be arrested and sent to prison for this breach of the law. That didn't happen. The rationing system was quite involved with stamps and little tokens that had to accompany all purchases of the rationed item. I am sure the process kept a lot of people employed and others frustrated. I think our car sticker was a capital B. That icon would allow Dad to purchase a certain amount of gasoline each month for the car. Also, the speed limit was set at thirty-five miles per hour on the open highway. That limit was meant to save gas and to remind everyone that we were at war.

On an occasion or two, I heard Mother tell the story about Dad making home brew during prohibition. This was before Mom and Dad became really involved in the church. She told us that something went wrong with some of his brew, and at night now and then a bottle would blow up. It made quite a racket, I guess. Mom was always afraid the law would come and arrest her and Dad, but I don't think it was illegal to make home brew. The problem began, I think, if one tried to sell it. Then it became a tax issue and a breaking of the law.

This old house was blessed with two porches, as stated before. The front porch was not used much. There was, however, a good swing on that porch, and all of us, from time to time, sat in it. It was on that porch and in that swing one summer evening that Mother was enjoying a few minutes of rest and relaxation when the swing gave way and broke. She landed on the floor, injuring her shoulder. I can still remember Dad helping her up, and the groans she made as she favored her shoulder. It was later discovered that one or more of my brothers had broken the swing earlier. They had put it back together with small, inconspicuous nails. That repair job gave way soon after Mother sat down. The fall's aftermath gave Mother much pain. Dad took her to a doctor in Marietta the next day. It was determined that no bones were broken, yet she suffered pain in that shoulder for the rest of her life.

The other porch, on the back side of the house, was screened in. It was always in use. In the summer it was used for preparing vegetables and fruit for canning. In cooler weather it was our refrigerator before we were able to get the real thing. Also, because of its metal roof, one could just sit out there to listen and enjoy the music as the rain played various tunes on the corrugated covering.

One fall when I was five, while my brothers were at school, I became aware that there were many watermelons left in a vegetable garden, which lay a major distance from the house. I decided to take my wagon and haul them in before they froze. I spent most of the afternoon bringing those melons in and placing them on the back porch. Mother profusely complimented me on my labor. She even told a neighbor or two about it, and that felt so good. Yes, the Hill work ethic was already being glorified, praised, and instilled in a preschooler.

Another memory from that back porch involves my great grandmother, Mary Bell Lovell Douglass, and my great grandfather, Charles L. Douglass, after whom I was named. I was quite young—a preschooler, although there was no preschool. The great grandparents were peeling peaches or apples. To liven things up a bit, I approached Great Grandpa with a toy gun in hand and yelled, "Bang, bang!" He was legally blind but could see some. He reached out and took hold of the little gun and said, "Don't ever point a gun at me or anyone else, ever." I was shocked. I didn't cry, but I was shocked.

It was wonderful advice. Guns can kill. In fact, in the United States around 40,000 people are killed annually by guns. It is a sad truth that few in government want to address this plague. Our Founding Fathers never dreamed that guns would be as great a threat to society as they are today. They shot guns that took time to reload. Today the 7.62mm Kalashnikov in automatic mode can fire about 600 rounds per minute.

Sooner or later, reasonable gun control must be enacted. Surely, thinking people will not let the killing go on forever. Yet for some politicians, if it means risking their greatly coveted jobs, they will continue to do nothing about this insanity. In April 2020, so-called militias stormed the Michigan State House. They carried handguns and high-powered assault rifles. That group, some of whom would later plot to kidnap the Governor, try her for treason, and then probably kill her, called themselves a militia. They are terrorists, and they should be treated as such. There are more than five hundred such groups in the United States. Most believe they are above the law or superior to the law. For what purpose do they exist? Certainly, with all the well-trained police we have in the land, there is no need for these trigger-happy groups. They are an ever-present safety threat to the general public. It is long past time for the government to pass legislation to eliminate them.

That very serious threat came to full fruition on January 6, 2021, when thousands of angry citizens, urged on by then President of the United States Donald J. Trump and others, invaded the Capitol Building in Washington D.C. This mob destroyed federal property and killed at least one policeman. One young woman was shot and killed by the police. She was pushing to get inside. Some of the mob were looking for the Vice President. They were angry at him for agreeing to fulfill his political responsibility and confirm the Electoral College's vote count. Others were searching for Nancy Pelosi, the Speaker of the House. Thank God the duly elected Senators and Representatives were not injured. But many of the President's party refused to find him responsible for urging a host of his followers to attack the Capitol.

Coming back to the porch, under one section was a cistern. Rainwater from the roof of the house and porch drained into that storage tank. The gathered rainwater was used for cooking and washing dishes. We even drank rainwater. I can still see Dad at the beginning of a thunderstorm, running out and turning a flap in a downspout so the run-off water would go onto the lawn. Once he felt the roof was clear of any dust and other debris, he closed the flap again, and the clean water ran into the cistern. But what happened when we were away and rains came? Looking back, I am grateful that we did not get sick from that water. Oh, it may have made us a bit ill from time to time, but it didn't kill us.

Monday was wash day. A farm family of six could create a lot of dirty laundry in a week's time. I can now sort clothes, throw them in the washer, set the dial, and return when they are done. Then I move them to the dryer, set the dial, and do whatever I want. When I hear the buzzer, I go back and finish with folding, etc. It wasn't that way at our house in Palmer Township. Cold water was carried to the wash house, and two big tubs sitting on a bench near the washing machine were each filled halfway. This was the rinse water. Once the clothing items were removed from the washer, they were put through the ringer, which consisted of two rubber rollers, one firm and one softer. The rollers squeezed out most of the soapy water. These pieces of clothing were then baptized in the first tub of rinse water and put through the ringer again. This action was repeated in the second tub. Finally, the items were run through the ringer one final time and deposited in a clothes basket. The clothes were then hung out on the clothesline to dry. Clothes that are dried in bright sun smell wonderful. But the sun was not always shining. On freezing days and rainy days, the wash was hung on temporary lines stretched across the screened-in porch, or wash day was put off until the weather cooperated. Home dryers were not heard of in those times, at least not in our neck of the woods. Had they been available, we could not have used them. Remember, we had neither natural gas nor electricity.

Filling the washing machine was a different story. The wash water had to be heated. And there was no hot water tank in the house. In summer the water was heated in a large copper kettle outside. In winter it was done on a small flat-top stove in the wash house. Once the water was hot, Dad would put it in the washer and Mother's clothes-washing day would begin—that is, if Dad could get the one-cylinder Maytag started. Remember, no electricity, so the washer had a two-cycle gasoline engine. That means the engine was lubricated by oil that was added to the gasoline. The engine was started with a foot pedal. Some days it took a lot of peddling to get that one-lung engine going. But once it started, the washer did the work.

Tuesday was bread baking day. There was nothing more pleasing to this growing boy than the smell of bread baking and knowing that I would soon get a slice of it. And of course, we often made our own butter, and that, spread on the warm bread, made any day seem like Christmas. With some of Mother's homemade peach jam or marmalade laced with bits of hickory nuts, the experience was perfect. The downside of the homemade bread was that it became crumbly after a few days. I was often envious of my fellow students at Palmer Elementary who brought sandwiches made with baker's bread. It didn't fall apart like the homemade.

The final room I will mention is the parlor. It was opened only on special days: when company was coming, or when it was a holy day like Christmas or Easter. Sometimes in summer, however, doors to the parlor and to the outside would be opened to assist air movement through the first floor, thus cooling the house. I can still remember one summer afternoon when I was about two years of age. The parlor doors were open to let the cool air pass through the house. I was playing on the floor, and Mom was in a huge rocker that matched the big couch that also folded out to make a bed. I can remember that Mom was rocking rather lively in that big chair when she suddenly stopped, came over and picked me up, hugged me close, and rocked me to sleep. What a warm memory.

Later on there was a piano in that room. The story of how we came to have that special instrument is almost unbelievable in today's context. It was a summer afternoon, and a small truck turned into our lane. It stopped beside the house, not far from the kitchen door. Two men exited the vehicle and threw back a canvas. On the truck was an upright piano.

One of the men said, "We heard that you might be interested in a piano." With that, one of the men climbed up on the truck and began to play some music. Mom and Dad talked a bit, then purchased the piano for fifty dollars. It stayed in the family for many years. I took lessons but never learned to play. I now regret that I did not take practicing seriously. My disregard for practice must have driven the teachers crazy.

There are many memories associated with that living room. The Christmas tree was always placed there. I can remember that some years there were very few decorations. Once or twice we strung popcorn together and decorated the tree with it. There were usually some bright bulbs, and icicles too, to make the tree more inviting. In those days we always cut our own Christmas tree from somewhere on the farm. There was, however, one Sunday afternoon in December when Dad, Mom, and a couple of us kids took a drive down toward Wolf Creek. Along the way we stopped by one farm where Christmas trees were being sold, or at least they were for sale. The price for a tree was twenty-five cents. I can still hear Mother saying, "Good heavens, twenty-five cents for a Christmas tree." The year of this event had to be 1936 or 1937; our Ford car was still fairly new.

One Christmas, Bob brought his girlfriend at the time, Genevieve Turner, to the house for Christmas dinner. She was a very pretty girl. Dad came into the room where Bob and Genevieve were sitting on the couch and greeted her warmly, then turned to Bob and said, "This isn't the girl you had here last time." To Dad it was a funny joke, but to Bob and Genevieve it was not funny at all. There had been no "last time" girl.

There is another image of that room, which is still in my mind. It was the first night after we received the telegram about brother Bob's death. The room was opened, the Aladdin lamp was providing illumination, and a fire had been lit in the stove, just in case someone came to share our grief. I was seated at a table that stood near the bay windows. With pencil and paper I began to write a poem about Bob and our pain. Whatever I had written remained on the table when I left the area. Later, I heard Mother telling someone about the poem. Whether I was gratified or embarrassed is a mystery.

Entertainment in those days was something we had to mostly create for ourselves. We did have a Victrola. It played only seventy-eight rpm records. I remember a couple of songs I liked most: "Maple on the Hill." It was a real tear-jerker. Also, "Golden Slippers." As you can guess, it moved swiftly. But the Victrola was not dependable. The spring broke often. Dad, after being prodded for a period of time, would put the machine's spring back together with small rivets. It would play a record or two and break again. There were no computers and no Amazon in those days, and it was not easy to secure parts. The record player was down most of the time. As I recall, a new spring was never purchased for the machine.

Many winter evenings were spent playing Chinese checkers. Six of us could play at a time. That meant at least two had to watch. Everyone, however, always had a chance to play. Mom and Dad taught us to share. Also, we had an English checkerboard, which was in play part of the time. The former was played with colored marbles and the latter with black and red chips. Sometimes we listened to our wet-cell battery radio. It was powered by an eight-volt car battery. The charge didn't last very long, and when it went dead, Dad had to take it to Beverly to get it charged again. When the battery was away, the radio didn't play. Later, Dad purchased a new dry-cell battery radio. It took three batteries. These units lasted much longer. But when they went dead, that was it. They were exported to the garbage heap, and Dad went back to Montgomery Ward for more.

Some evenings one of the family members would pop popcorn. It took several skillets of popped corn to satisfy the whole group—a family of six. Also, there were always apples to be brought up from the cellar. Apples in those days could be purchased over at the Experiment Farm near Fleming, Ohio, for a dollar or less a bushel. Dad and Mom usually purchased several bushels in the fall, enough to last through the winter. When company came, conversation, apples, and popcorn were usually the refreshments. Yes, kids, I know that all sounds quaint and dull, but it was the way we lived, and life was enjoyable without all the stuff that clutters our every waking hour today. In recent years I have watched as two people sit at a table in a restaurant. Each focuses on his or her cell phone. They completely ignore each other unless they are texting each other in lieu of engaging in real face-to-face conversation. It's enough to drive an old-timer mad.

Some of the radio programs that we listened to regularly were *Henry Aldrich, Fibber McGee and Molly, The Great Gildersleeve, My Miss Brooks,* and more. We also, on Saturday night, listened to *The Grand Old Opry* from WSM, Nashville, Tennessee. Some of the entertainers I remember were Uncle Dave Macon, Roy Acuff, Ernest Tubb, and Bradley Kincaid. During the day, Mother listened to a soap or two. One she listened to faithfully was *Just Plain Bill*. I still remember the guitar theme music. As I recall, the plot of the soap revolved around a lumberyard. And the *Bill* was *Bill Davidson*. Many evenings a passage of scripture was read and a prayer given before we all ambled off to bed.

The Wheeling, West Virginia, radio station, WWVA, carried many country and western entertainers. A couple I remember were Lulu Belle and Scotty. They were husband and wife. Another was Cowboy Lowy. I still remember a few lines of his theme song:

> *Banners are flying, today's the big show,*
> *Cowboys are whooping the big rodeo.*
> *The announcers are busy, the horns give a toot,*
> *Cowboys rush dogies to the end of the shoot.*

I haven't said much about family summer entertainment. Truth is, we often worked all day, ate supper, and then went back to work. Oh, yes, on the farm our evening meal was always supper. Dinner was at noon. After supper came milking time, and if there was still daylight remaining, somewhere there was more work to be done. And when the darkness closed the summer day, we often gathered on the concrete patio outside the kitchen door. There we reviewed the day's activities and talked about what work would be done tomorrow. We would also discuss any news that had been picked up on the party line phone or the radio. Sometimes the wonderful smell of freshly cut sweet clover would drift across the area where we were relaxing. What a wonderful aroma. Lightning bugs would fire up the night over in the apple orchard just across the lane. Some evenings Dick and I would put some of those bugs in glass jars and use them to light our way around the yard. Poor lightning bugs.

Radio news was always important. Mom listened to it faithfully. Two names I recall were Walter Winchell and Gabriel Heatter. The latter always came on with either: "Ah, there is good news tonight," or "Ah, there is bad news tonight." It all depended on how the war was going. Winchell's greeting began with the clicking sound of telegraph keys at work and then this: "Good evening, Mr. and Mrs. America, from border to border and coast to coast and all the ships at sea." He had been a showman in vaudeville, and his delivery reflected something of his showmanship.

I do remember a few nights when our Beckner cousins from the Bingham farm up the road came down, and we ended up in the yard, gazing up at the glorious heavens. It was amazing how beautiful the night sky was in that place. There were no electric lights in the community. When darkness came, it was DARK. And with the darkness so complete, the heavens shown like expensive diamonds floating in a beautiful sea of blue. We would find the Big Dipper and the Little, too. We always tried to find the North Star. I am not certain that we knew it then, but that star had guided many souls along the Underground Railroad to freedom in the North. Looking back, all I can say is how wonderful it was to have those early experiences with nature, up close and personal. Of course, most all life was "up close and personal" on that farm.

THE HOUSE

There was another form or two of entertainment in which we engaged from time to time in winter. The first was ice cream making. Chunks of ice would be cut out of the frozen creek and brought up to the house. Those ice chunks would then be broken up into smaller pieces. Mom would mix the milk, sugar, eggs, and vanilla. That mixture was then poured into the cylindrical metal container and placed in the wooden freezer. Next came the ice and salt. Adding salt assisted in the freezing process. We then turned the crank until it could be turned no longer. It was very important to keep open the freezer drain, which was near the top, so salt water could run out. If salt water got into the container of ice cream, it was ruined. When the work was completed, we all enjoyed a great treat.

Another activity in which the whole family engaged was taffy making. Mother would prepare a sugar-laden mixture on the stove. When the texture was just right and cooled some, each of us would be given a blob of it. We would then pull it and stretch it. Sometimes the stretching went on for several minutes. It sometimes seemed like hours to me. And when the color and texture were just right, it was time to let it rest for a bit. And then the greatest joy of all began—eating it. I could use some now. Side note: Mother always made sure we had washed our hands before she gave us any of the mixture to pull.

It was wonderful to have four cousins just up the road. We visited back and forth regularly. I was up there one afternoon when a sudden summer thunderstorm hit. It was a gully washer. Lightning filled the sky and thunder shook the whole house. Aunt Helen got all of us kids into a corner near the door that led upstairs. The harsh intruder made the place shake, rattle, and roll, but it finally passed. When I went home, a half mile or so, there was a lot of activity in the house. Lightning had run in on the phone line and blew the phone off the wall. The front door had been open, and I was told a ball of fire went out through it. There was a lot of cleanup to do. Both lath and plaster lay on the floor. The good news was that the strike did not start a fire. In those days, a house fire out in the countryside was rarely extinguished. It burned until the building and everything in it were totally consumed.

One evening my family and I were visiting with the Beckner family. Uncle George was there too. I do not recall just where I was in the house when I heard a lot of scurrying around in the kitchen. When I made it to that room, Uncle was being held on a chair by two people, and his body was going through many strange contortions. Someone yelled, "Get a wooden spoon to put in his mouth to keep him from biting himself." In a few minutes he came out of the seizure and appeared normal but exhausted. It was then that I learned what an epileptic seizure looked like. Uncle George, Mother's brother, died in his early fifties. He died from bladder cancer. Most of us believe that the very strong medication he took to prevent seizures caused the malignancy. Sometimes that which is supposed to help us can also kill us.

One freeze-framed moment I carry in my mind was indelibly etched there on a Christmas morning, probably 1937, the first Christmas the Beckners lived up the road from us. That picture is of Aunt Helen and Uncle Tom coming through the kitchen door with snow all over them. They were carrying a wash tub filled with food items. Aunt Helen and Mom, I am sure, had arranged for our families to share Christmas dinner together. It had snowed about six inches during the night. Uncle Tom didn't want to risk getting his big old Studebaker stuck in the snow, so Uncle Tom and Aunt Helen just walked down. It was less than a mile. Of course, following Uncle and Aunt were their four children. We enjoyed a great day together.

In fact, we enjoyed many good times together. One Fourth of July an ice-cream freezer was borrowed from the Palmer Ladies Aid, and we made three gallons of ice cream. I suppose there was other food, but I don't remember that. In those days ice cream was a treat we seldom had. Today there are always two or three flavors in our freezer. It is still a wonderful dessert. I could consume ice cream morning, noon, and night. But I try to limit myself.

PART TWO

BEYOND THE HOUSE

CHAPTER 2

THE ORCHARD

ACROSS THE DRIVEWAY there was a small orchard where most every spring we gathered sweet apples and later, cider apples. The sweet apples were not good for cooking, so I was told. They were, however, wonderful to eat raw. Often the cider apples contained a bit of extra protein, yet the cider was tasty, and we never really thought much about a worm or two.

Some hogs also kept residence in the orchard, at least during the summer. They were beneficial in keeping the grass under control and the snakes at bay. And they were close enough to the house that we didn't have too far to carry the kitchen scraps. Leftover items from the kitchen were fed to the swine. I often laughed at how those pigs fought over the slop. They were our real-live garbage disposal units. In the shelter-in-place order during the Coronavirus epidemic, when people fought over toilet paper in the aisles of our grocery stores, I thought about those pigs fighting over slop. Humanity sometimes does mimic lower animal behavior. And, on second thought, not just during pandemics.

The orchard also contained a low area through which stormwater ran off and emptied into the creek below. Many times during summer thunderstorms, water backed up into that field. This occurred because the lane leading over to the house was built up, and the culvert through which the water from the field had to exit was just too small to do the job when a storm hit. As a child I found it quite amazing to see the lake form and then in a few minutes disappear. Sometimes it is a come-and-go world. Life often presents us with now-you-see-it, now-you-don't kinds of experiences.

Also, I remember at least one wiener roast held at the edge of that orchard. It was a small gathering of people from the Waterford Nazarene Church. Climbing over the fence was a problem for some. But the staples held the fence secure as we climbed over to the other side. No one was injured. I now wonder just where the hogs were during that social gathering. Interesting.

CHAPTER 3

THE BARN

EVERY FARM HAS A BARN. At least in those days that was true. Ours was a hillside structure. The upper part stored hay, and the lower level housed the bovines and equines. Sometimes pigs too. I remember some evenings when I accompanied Dad as he husked corn by lantern light on that barn floor between the hay mows that were on either side. He didn't work by lantern light often. I suppose that is one reason I remember it so clearly. Of course, every morning and every evening we were in the barn, for cows must be milked twice a day, and we did it. Later some dairies milked three times a day, but I think the law of diminishing returns dictated that the practice be discontinued.

Above I mentioned the residents of the barn. There was one very large sow that was housed in a pen there when she was about to farrow. The sow was white and huge. She produced, I believe, sixteen offspring. Dad was ecstatic. All those lovely young pigs. What a large litter! But the ecstasy was short lived. She ate most, if not all, of them. What a disappointment. It was just unbelievable. That event was in several ways a catastrophe. First there was the destruction of the piglets. Second, the lost income those pigs would have produced. And finally, the sow had to be sold because she could no longer be trusted to produce more offspring.

It seems humorous to me now. I was so eager to milk cows when I was a child that at the beginning, Mother or someone gave me a very large tin cup to use for that work. I suppose it held about a quart. Upon reflection, I have a feeling there was a lot of laughter behind my back.

I do remember one evening after a day of thrashing. The wheat had been brought on wagons from the field into an area near the barn and fed into the machine that separated the wheat from the straw. We were probably a bit late with the milking. At one point someone looked up and saw a six-foot-long black snake slithering along one of the joists that supported the upper floor. I suppose this beautiful reptile had taken a ride into the area on one of the farm wagons. He had probably been secluded in a sheaf of wheat. He discovered too late that he was in the wrong place at the wrong time. My brother Bill, who seemed always quick on the trigger, ran to the house, got the .22 rifle, and shot it dead. Today we would not kill a black snake. Black snakes can frighten a person, but they are not dangerous. In fact, they are good to have around. They control mice and such, but they can scare a person half to death when they appear suddenly and are not expected.

In summertime, cows ran in the pasture field during the day. After being milked in the evening, they would be turned back out to pasture. Usually in the morning they were standing in the lane, waiting for their humans to come and milk them. They would, however, on occasion, not come in. It was then that our collie dog would be sent to compel them. About all we had to say to the dog was, "Go get 'em," and he went quickly. Sometimes in the evening the cows would not come in by themselves, and the dog, once again, would be sent to escort them up the lane to the barn.

Dogs were a great help on the farm back then. And they not only continue to do that kind of work today, but now they help humanity in so many other ways. Dogs, at least some, are very smart and can be taught to do police work and recovery work when disasters hit. They can sniff out illegal drugs and some illnesses. They can be guides to persons with special needs and, of course, bring joy to millions of people as pet members of our families.

In winter, the situation was different. The cows were kept in or near the barn all day. They were fed hay and given shelter from the weather. And when we were milking, the cows were fed silage topped with ground, enriched grain. Of course, with the cows being kept in the barn most of the time in winter, the result was that, come spring, the barn floor where they stayed was several inches deep with straw and manure. That buildup of waste material had to be hauled away or the animals would ultimately be forced to enter the barn on their knees. As would their human tenders.

One of my first memories of spending extra time with my dad was when he was cleaning the barn in early spring. The process was simple. Bring the manure spreader into the barn through double doors, which allowed such entrance. Then with a pitchfork, usually with four tines (prongs), engage some of that murky substance. Pull it loose from where it was packed down and throw it into the spreader. When the spreader was full, the horses would pull it out to the field. Dad would set a lever that put a chain drive in motion, and that chain drive would move crossbars that pushed the barn material slowly toward the back. There, beaters shredded the manure, threw it high into the air, and distributed it over a wide area. Then the manure would drop to the ground.

Manure was good fertilizer, and it is still used as such. This process, however, has now become problematic in many areas. A heavy rain runoff causes the nutrients to produce algae in some of our lakes and streams and raises the risk of fouling the water supply that is so crucial to the wellbeing of the citizens who live in our towns and cities. Toledo, Ohio, has experienced some major problems with algae due to runoff into Lake Erie.

Some might think it strange, but Dad found a way to let me ride on the spreader with him. The seat where the driver sat was not large enough for two. So he would put some clean straw on top of the manure, and I would sit there until there was space to stand in the spreader. As the spreader unloaded, the cross bars in the bottom of the machine moved the waste material very slowly toward the back, thus creating a space where I could stand. These cross bars moved so slowly I could safely step over them as they moved along. My balance was maintained by holding onto Dad or the front of the spreader. It was great fun and even more so because I was with my dad. Once I was tired of this manure spreading, I am sure a good nap followed at the house. And I suppose Mother, like any good parent, thought little of the perfume I brought with me upon entering.

There are a host of memories from things I did in or near that old barn. One of the first that stands out in my mind could have meant the end of my life, or at least could have crippled me forever. Dad, standing in the kitchen one morning, was telling Mom about a nest of baby owls in the top of the silo. He called them monkey-faced owls (they were probably barn owls). I was about five years of age. The thought of how neat it would be to see owls like he was describing prodded me to go take a look. It was quite easy to enter the silo near its top if one did it from the hay mow. All I needed to do was move through an opening from the top of the hay mow that provided access to the top of the silo. Somehow I was able to move close enough to see this nest of the most beautiful and interesting, fluffy young birds one could imagine. I fully enjoyed what my eyes beheld. The birds' faces were spectacular. But I never ever told my parents what I had done (not even after I grew up). I thought it might frighten them. It frightens me now, as I look down that thirty-foot shaft over which I was maneuvering my five-year-old body. Sometimes kids are simply fearless—or a bit insane. Maybe both.

Another time, in late summer, I suppose, Dick and I were in the garden one morning about ten o'clock. I do not recall why we were there. I have a feeling Mom or Dad had given us an assignment. We were in the watermelon patch. We decided to pull one of those melons to see if it was any good. We took it up to the barn floor where we broke it open.

THE BARN

It was absolutely the best, sweetest melon I think I have ever tasted. We marveled at its unique flavor as it exploded in our mouths. But there were two problems: we were not hungry at lunchtime, and we couldn't tell anyone how good the watermelon was. Most decisions need to be thoroughly thought through before one embraces them. Of course, if we always did that, we might miss some of the most exciting and enlightening moments of life. Also, we might avoid moments of behavior that call for confession and repentance.

One spring day, maybe around 1940, a storm went through Palmer Township while my brothers and I were at Palmer Elementary. The sky darkened and Miss Wilma Nieb asked Kay Pugh, a fourth-grader who, I believe, was the custodian, to light the lanterns that hung from the ceiling. There was a lot of wind and rain. I recall that as we headed home, a field near the M. E. (Methodist Episcopal) Church looked like a lake. Water everywhere. When we boys arrived home, we gradually sensed that something was different. It took a while. As we walked up the lane and pondered the scene, suddenly someone shouted, "The silo is gone." And sure enough, it was. It had been twisted off its foundation and lay shattered on the ground. Dad and Mom thought it may have been a small tornado that did it. They had seen those kinds of storms when they lived in Kansas and Oklahoma.

Mom told a story of the first tornado they experienced in Oklahoma. "We lived in a lease house owned by the oil company for which Dad worked," she said. "We knew there was a storm cellar, but we stayed in the house as the storm approached. The wind was so strong that we had to physically, with our bodies, hold the front door shut. We could see the wooden oil derricks falling all over the area," she continued. "It was a really frightening experience. We were not injured, but next time as a storm rolled in, we knew to head for the storm cellar."

I am certain our silo was hit by a tornado. That conclusion is predicated upon the twisted debris pattern as it lay scattered on the ground.

Also, I have a feeling that if the silo had been full, it would have survived. It was rebuilt before fall silo-filling time. Good as new, although with a few replacement staves. Yes, the silo was of wooden stave construction, held together by strong steel hoops.

A few years ago, in a sermon given at Yellow Springs United Methodist Church, I told the story of how the wind destroyed the silo. I hadn't thought much about it for years—actually, for scores of years. But as I struggled for a meaningful illustration of how to maintain life when the winds of this world are threatening our very existence, the silo image suddenly appeared to me. It was Friedrich Nietzsche who said, "He who has a why to live for can bear almost any how." Viktor Frankl wrote something like that in his little book *Man's Search for Meaning*. If a life has inner substance, it can stand firm against almost any life-threatening destructive force. To believe in some force bigger than ourselves is a great help in the time of stress.

There was a special moment in the backyard that has stayed in my mind now for more than seventy-five years. For some reason I was up near an old building that was used by Dad as a workshop. I was probably twenty feet from it. There was a large Dominique hen wandering around kind of looking for whatever she could see, I suppose. Suddenly her head went down into the grass, and when it came up, she had a small snake clamped tightly in her beak. The snake must have been nearly a foot long. I was amazed. I watched. The snake was slim, but the chicken still had to wrestle with it for what seemed to me a very long time. This little snake was not going to become hen food if he could help it. He could not help it. The hen finally got it all swallowed. I thought to myself, *She will have a great story to tell her hen friends at their next pecking party.* She could tell them, "I swallowed the whole thing." It did seem to me that as she tried to conquer that wiggly creature, she had a very puzzled look on her face, like she was saying, "I have never seen a night crawler this resistant." Sometimes in rural life one sees the strangest things. And of course, strange stuff is not limited just to rural areas. In fact, a lot of stuff in today's world—whether in the city or the countryside—seems super strange to me.

Up the lane toward the barn was a place where a large horse-drawn sled sat when not in use, which was most of the time. One summer day I decided to learn to ride the family bicycle. I was able to stand on the runner of that old sled and mount the bike. I am not certain now just how far I was able to go on my first attempt. Not far, I am sure. But I was not about to be denied. I kept trying. Finally the two-wheeler stayed up, and I made it down the lane several hundred feet. Yet, I really hadn't learned how to control the thing. It headed for the fence enclosing the orchard. The bike and I crashed into that woven-wire fence. I picked myself and the bike up, and we headed back to the sled. Within an hour or two I was able to ride, control, and stop where I wanted. But to be totally honest, I did hit that fence several times before I learned how to stop when I wanted to. One more life-limiting obstacle conquered, somewhat.

Many years later, I watched our daughter Elizabeth go through the same struggle one afternoon. It was bushes in which she landed again and again. Finally I saw her peddling across the lawn with a smile on her face. She too had conquered this two-wheeled beast.

Within a few feet of where that Dominique swallowed the snake, stood our one-car garage. It was quite small. To access the car, one needed to open the doors and block them from closing of their own freewill. Learning to drive was a special dream from very early in my life, I guess. One evening, when the family was going somewhere, I decided I would back the car out of the building. I knew how to start the car and put it in reverse. Then, like a truck driver or two I had seen, I opened the driver's door just a little, looked back, and let out on the clutch. All was going very well until the door caught on the side of the building. The accident must have produced some noise, for in a few minutes Dad came and rescued me from the car. The car door was bent some. Dad straightened it out the best he could, but a portion of the car door carried a few tell-tale marks from that day on.

ROLLING HILLS

Later, maybe a year, maybe less, the car was parked just outside the garage. We were, again, going someplace as a family. We were all dressed up. I was outside early and decided to turn the Ford around and head it out the lane. It had to have been early fall, for nearby was a rather large pile of freshly sawed firewood. Now you, as the reader, know something bad is about to happen. I was able to get the vehicle almost turned, but something went wrong, and the front end of the car landed partway up the side of that woodpile. Again, Dad came quickly out the door and retrieved the car. No damage done as far as I can recall. I think there was a rather stern directive to cease and desist from trying to drive. I didn't drive again until the second farm when I was thirteen, then sometimes I drove back to the pasture field to herd the milk cows toward the barn. I wasn't on the highway, but I was driving.

Just a short distance from the garage was our brooder house. Sometimes it was used as a smokehouse in which we cured ham and bacon. Yet it was used every year as a place to nurture newly hatched chicks for a few weeks. Our chicks almost always arrived by way of the United States Postal Service. That may seem strange, but that is the way it was. When the local mail carrier delivered the chicks, he brought them over to the house so they would not be left out in the cold. These chicks were in boxes of one hundred. The box contained four sections, and there were twenty-five chicks in each part. These young chicks were brought into the brooder house in the big cardboard containers. We took them out one at a time, gave each one a drink of water and the offer of some starter mash. Starting at the age of five, I was invited to help with giving the chicks a bit of water and mash. Most of the time one or two would be dead, suffocated.

It was crucial that the place remain quite warm for the chicks. That was achieved with help from a kerosene heater equipped with a large hood that rested close to the floor. The chicks could stay close to the heat as long as they wanted, and then they could move closer to the outside if they wished for a cooler environment. It was amazing to watch how quickly the chicks grew. In a few weeks they would be released to run outside in a fenced area. Most of our chickens were allowed to reach maturity and were used to provide eggs for eating and selling. The roosters in the group were usually used for Sunday dinner.

CHAPTER 4

MY HUNDRED ACRES OF ADVENTURE SPACE

THERE WAS ONE LATE SUMMER afternoon when, for some reason now lost to memory, I took my collie dog, Old Prince, and headed down the lane that led from the barn to the pasture field. At the end of the lane, we crossed a small swampy stream. A foot log aided in that endeavor. We then went out past a huge sycamore tree and on east to a beautiful white oak standing stately above the valley below. There I sat down and feasted my eyes on that valley, especially the creek we had just crossed. It was a perfect day with a warm breeze filtering across the landscape. Fall colors began to hint of change that was on the way. Old Prince found a place a few feet away and lay down to rest. But there was a noisy distraction overhead. My dog became restless. He looked up and turned his head this way and that, wondering what in the world was up there. I knew what it was: squirrels. They were chattering loudly, and from time to time they dropped acorns around us intruders. I don't remember how long we stayed there. I do know this: across the years when my life has been stressful, I found solace in recalling that beautiful afternoon my dog and I spent under a great oak tree, high on a knoll above that placid valley and stream. I am fully aware today that there are too few such memorable moments to bless most of our adult lives. We need more of those relaxing, quiet times.

There were times when we used certain parts of that stream that flowed below the knoll as a place to swim. It wasn't wide or deep enough for proper swimming. None of us could swim anyway. But we could get wet and be cool when the weather was hot. I remember Mother warning us to stay out of the creek during the dog days of August. "That water will make you sick," she would say.

Another memory of that creek is a winter scene. I do not know where one of my brothers secured an old pair of clamp-on ice skates. Even now I can see some of us trying to use them one afternoon on that creek when it was frozen solid. I don't think I was ever able to stand up on those skates. And I don't think my brothers were successful either. When I see professional skaters on TV, it amazes me to see how they can move so gracefully on those blades. It looks so easy. And yet, I know for the untrained it is a nearly impossible endeavor even to stand up on them. Later I would become able to stay up on roller skates, but I didn't master even that art. I was kind of a klutz, I guess, at least on skates.

My brothers and I also fished in that little creek. One summer when our Aunt Hattie Ormiston and Cousin Bruce were visiting from Michigan, my brothers and Cousin Bruce decided to go fishing. Everyone had a pole, line, and hook but me. I thought they were going to leave me out of that adventure. My aunt, however, was quite creative. She found a safety pin, bent it into a fishhook shape, put it on a string, and then helped me find a stick for the pole. I went fishing with the big boys. I didn't catch anything, but I was a part of the gang. And I have found that in life, for me, belonging to the group is often the best part.

I have spoken of my Aunt Hattie a number of times. She was a registered nurse. She was working at that profession when she met her husband. He, I think, had been injured in an auto accident, and she was assigned to his case. He was a young widower, and during his hospital stay he must have decided that she would make a good wife. He was twenty-eight and she was thirty-one and never married. The record shows that they were wed in the Gilman Avenue Methodist Church, Marietta, Ohio, Saturday, March 2, 1929. She was special in many ways.

Mother told me that when I was several weeks old, I weighed less than when I was born. Aunt Hattie and Uncle Roland (Hoolie was his nickname) came to visit. My dear aunt told Mother that I was starving. Mother's breast milk was not sufficient. So, believe it or not, that very day I was put on raw cow's milk. I suppose it could have killed me, but instead I grew.

There is another very clear memory that involves that aunt. I was a little less than four years of age. For some reason, my family was visiting with Aunt Hattie. Dad and my brothers went back to the Palmer farm, but Mom and I stayed with Aunt Hattie. I don't remember Uncle being there. He was an oil field worker and may have been away. It was January 1937. The Ohio and Muskingum Rivers were raging. Aunt Hattie lived on Harmer Hill. Sometime the next day my dad and brothers returned, and we all went out to a spot that overlooked the rivers. I remember two things about that experience: I was directed not to slide down some stone or step, and I observed a two-story house floating down the Muskingum and lodging against a bridge. That house against the bridge is still clear in my mind. I recall it being blue.

Now let me return to the creek. There is one more scene that appeared to me as I recalled that ice-skating adventure. Not far from where we tried skating was another large tree. I cannot remember whether it was an oak or curly maple. It could have been poplar. Uncle George, Mother's brother mentioned above, was visiting us for a while. One afternoon he invited my brothers and me to take a walk back across the farm. He was probably dealing with some pressing life issue (he had many) and wanted to breathe some fresh air and think. Everything was going fine until one of those sudden Midwest summer thunderstorms came roaring over the hills. Uncle

ROLLING HILLS

George led us to shelter under that tree. The storm passed, we didn't get too wet, and in a little while we were back at the house. It was only later that I learned a person should never seek shelter under a tree during thunderstorms. I don't know whether Uncle George knew the danger or not. Truth is, we survived. For that fact I am grateful. Had it been a walnut or locust, which have taproots and draw lightning, we might not have been so lucky.

Today, much of the above-mentioned creek exists only in my mind. Many years ago the owners of the farm had a dam built near the big oak, under which the dog and I spent some special time. The footbridge, a portion of the creek where my brothers and I fished, and some of the pasture field are now under several feet of water.

Everything in this world changes, sometimes by the hand of humans and sometimes by time and circumstance. So much history is hidden from our contemporary eyes. Sometimes it is buried beneath us, and sometimes it is hiding in plain sight. We pass by on our way to some very important appointment and fail to remember that others traveled this way before we came along. I should never forget that truth, for when I was a child on that farm, we often found arrowheads in the fields as we worked. Others were here long before we white Anglo Saxons came, believing we had discovered a new world. The land was here all the time, and those who owned it before us were forced westward by the invading hoards from Europe.

President Andrew Jackson was one of the worst abusers. Thousands died as the result of his forced Trail of Tears—his order to clear the indigenous people out of the homes they had known for generations and drive them to the Oklahoma Territory. And after they were moved out, Jackson practically gave their land to rich southern plantation owners who then imported Black slaves from Virginia and other places to grow cotton. These enslaved people created billions of dollars in wealth for their owners and did not receive one red cent for it, nor did their progeny gain anything for all that labor. It went to white people.

MY HUNDRED ACRES OF ADVENTURE SPACE

Some Americans today still live high on the hog due to the wealth created by our enslaved Black brothers and sisters during those unspeakably cruel and heartless centuries. And still there is great prejudice in the land toward Black persons who are here. God help us to recognize that the Black people did not choose to come to this land. They were brought here in chains. They have contributed so much to this country, and they are still contributing, but are harassed constantly—sometimes subtly and sometimes quite openly.

Mitch McConnell, who blocked President Obama from appointing a super balanced jurist to the Supreme Court, did what a racist would gladly have done. Yes, I believe he and some other senators did their best to punish Obama for living in the White House while being Black. They seem to love the President who followed him, even though that man was anathema to decency and democracy. The Senate had an opportunity to remove him from office, but the majority were afraid they might lose their next election. The November 2020 election determined that Donald Trump's reign would end on January 20, 2021. Mr. Trump refused to concede that Joe Biden won and urged some of his super supporters to march on the Capitol and overthrow the election. They did. They wrecked the place. They made fools of themselves, damaged our democracy, but did not change the election. And following that rebellion, the House of Representatives impeached Mr. Trump, again. He is the only President to be impeached twice. Now the ex-president faces years of time interfacing with law courts.

Well, I digressed, so now I will return to Palmer Township in the 1930s and '40s. There was always something to explore on that farm. A few acres of it were covered in woods. There were all kinds of trees, large and small, hardwood and soft. In summer, cattle of the non-milking type were placed in the field where the wooded area was. Thus, there were inviting paths made by the bovines. Often my dog and I would explore that part of the farm. The woods provided my family with firewood, which was used for both cooking and heating. And now, as I write this, I recall using some of the stumps there as my pulpit. Yes, preachers were the only great men (chuckle, chuckle) I was exposed to. So, in my mind, I became a preacher. Isn't that a scream? Starting in my twenty-fourth year, preaching is the life's work I have followed now for more than sixty years. I committed myself to carrying on the work of my grandfathers and uncles who were self-taught clergy. I just took it a little further.

Also, often while walking through those woods I would come across a land turtle. Land turtles are harmless. Sometimes I would pick the turtle up and closely look it over. On occasion in those days, one might find a turtle with someone's initials carved on it. In those woods there were also initials carved on several of the trees. It seems that we all want to be forever remembered, one way or another.

Speaking of using trees for firewood, there was a related event that gave pause to Mom, Dad, and the rest of the family. It happened one day when Dad and my older brothers were sawing firewood. The saw was circular, maybe three feet in diameter. A tree limb would be laid up on a moveable table that allowed the person in charge to push the tree limb forward and saw off a section about eighteen inches in length. The sawed section would then drop to the ground. It was important to keep the severed pieces away from the sawblade as it turned.

One afternoon, Bill was throwing the pieces away from the saw and tossing them into a pile. He must have lost focus for a second, and momentarily, his arm came very close to the sawblade. His arm came so close that the blade cut his jacket sleeve at the wrist. The teeth of the blade did not touch his skin, but Bill must have felt the vibration. Mom and I were going to West Virginia that afternoon with Aunt Helen and Uncle Tom. We were almost there when Uncle Tom told Mom what had happened. She was quite upset. But Uncle reminded her that the sawing had stopped before we left the house. She remembered and was relieved.

Near that wooded area on the backside of the farm was a persimmon grove. Every fall when the fruit of the trees ripened, we boys would go back there and pick up a few persimmons and eat them. If one of us bit into a green one, we reflexively spit it out. Unripe persimmons would pucker the mouth and make the eyes water. The raccoon in the area also liked the persimmons. There was a lot of evidence supporting that conclusion. The signs were everywhere.

In a ravine nearby grew a tall woody bush that was something like bamboo. The stalks of this plant would grow ten or fifteen feet high, maybe higher. I don't know whether it was good for much of anything or not. It was soft in the middle and could easily be hollowed out. It made great whistles and pop guns. We called it stinkwood because it exuded a strange odor. I do think we used that wood to make drains for extracting sap from maple trees. That sap was boiled down to make maple syrup.

Not far from the stinkwood and the persimmon grove was a line fence between our farm and some neighboring land. There was, just across that fence, a wild plum grove. I don't think we ever climbed the fence to pick or eat any of that wild fruit. But the grove I remember. And many years ago, when life must have been bearing down on me once more, I paused from my work and transferred my thoughts into the following words:

> I walked this week
> back the crooked dusty lane
> that runs from the old hillside barn
> to the wild plum grove
> that hugs a weather-beaten fence
> where two farms run together.
> I tiptoed through the autumn woods
> where giant old oaks red and white
> reach out and touch each other
> with entwined arms strong as steel.

ROLLING HILLS

> And I helped saw some wood
> that will keep us warm when the
> winter winds blow cold.
> And I ran with Ole Prince
> the big collie dog who knows the cows by name,
> and almost fell off the old foot log again
> that crosses the creek near the foot of the lane.
> And as I did all this,
> I thought to myself, Remembering is bliss. (1975)

There were some wild animals on that farm. Mostly there were rabbits and squirrels. During hunting season we hunted them and used them for food. Mother would roll the various parts in flour and fry them in a skillet. Some of the meat tasted a lot like chicken. We did not have rabbit hounds, so it was more difficult to bag the rabbits. Yet, if three or four men were to spread out across the field, chances were we would flush out a rabbit.

One day the Nazarene preacher from Waterford was on the hunting team. Suddenly a rabbit jumped up and took off in double time. The minister yelled, "There he goes, there he goes!" I don't think that rabbit stopped to see who was reporting his rapid takeoff.

One of the by-products of a squirrel hunt was the tail. Young men and not-so-young men would tie them to the radio aerials on their cars. I have seen as many as five or six tails on some vehicles. It was some kind of mark that announced greatness. To have that many tails on your car was evidence that one was a high achiever.

During the years I was growing up in Palmer, I never saw a deer. There just were no deer there. The men who hunted deer went to West Virginia or Pennsylvania to hunt. I have a feeling that in about 1950, either during hunting season or not, my brother-in-law bagged a deer or two. Whether in season or out. Today there are so many deer in my state that thousands are killed annually by motor vehicles. Also, because housing development has pushed into the deer habitat, some cities, like Columbus, Ohio, have found it necessary to thin the herds so hundreds of deer will not starve.

My brothers did set traps for racoons. At one time I think a pelt was worth four or five dollars. The brothers used steel traps that kept the animal from getting away. I suppose once they approached a live animal, they killed it. Some nights we heard the coon hunters at their art. The bark and wail of a coon hound when he has treed one of those animals is a unique sound. There is nothing quite like it. I mentioned the leghold trap. They are very cruel. One day my brothers were running their traps and found a trap with a raccoon's foot. The animal had wanted to free itself, and that was the only way he could do it. Think about that process a bit. Sad.

There were also weasels and foxes and skunks on that farm. If a weasel got into the chicken house, it could kill a lot of chickens in a short period of time. Some neighbors suffered loss of chickens by weasels, but I don't remember that my family had such bad luck. Skunks were always around. And when they were around, they let us know they were present. On an occasion or two some of the older Palmer Elementary boys who hunted would find themselves confronted by a skunk. Sometimes they were sprayed before they could escape. On a number of occasions one or two of those boys came to school with their hunting clothes on. Wow! Of course, back in those days, some of the boys may have had just one pair of pants. Such memories!

CHAPTER 5

PLANTING SEASON

ON THIS FARM IN THE 1930S, our only real power source was two moderate sized gray mares. The mares did the heavy lifting. They were horses that had run wild in the west, were captured and brought back to Ohio and sold. They were high spirited and could deliver a lot of energy. Sometimes they did not want to come to the barn, be harnessed, and go work in the fields. One day as brother Bill was bringing them in, they broke and ran away just as he was trying to move them up the lane. Finally, he went to the house and retrieved our .410 gauge shotgun. He was once again able to get them to the lane opening. There they stopped as before. He shot one or both in the behind. He didn't judge the distance perfectly. Some of the buckshot stayed glued to their skin. When Dad learned what had happened, he inspected the team and found the buckshot. Bill was directed to go curry the horses until the lead was all off their hide. I don't think the horses ever broke and ran again. He taught them a highly effective lesson. Needless to say, not in a humane manner.

We also had a small black and white pony that had worked in coal mines. He was blind. He was mostly a pet, but on occasion he was used to cultivate the garden. We called him Tony. A man once came and asked if the pony was for sale. I was infuriated when I discovered the purpose of the man's visit. I used a few of the words I learned from our neighbor. But Dad knew how much Tony was a part of the family and told the man Tony was not for sale.

One Saturday night Garland Townsend came home with us, and when morning came, he wanted to see the pony. We found Tony down in the pasture field, and Garland got on him. It was a kind of humorous sight, for the boy was tall, and his feet almost touched the ground. But Tony took it all in stride and carried him along.

Eventually we boys outgrew this beautiful animal, and we sold him to Newman Ford, the man who picked up our milk each morning and took it to the United Dairy at Waterford. I agreed to ride Tony about six miles to Ford's farm. Because of the pony's blindness, he had a fear of going downhill. So as I rode him along township, county, and state roads for that six miles, occasionally I had to dismount, take the reins in hand, and lead him down the hill. I am sure Tony never heard a harsh word from me that day. We may have sold him, but he was still an animal we loved. Mr. Ford's two little boys probably learned to love him too. I hope he had a good life.

The vegetable garden was essential to our family. Early in spring the peas, lettuce, and radishes were the first to be planted and the first to produce. About the same time that these early staples were planted, so were the potatoes. The potatoes were to be in the ground by St. Patrick's Day. Potatoes are tough and resistant to frost. In May the tomato plants were set out, usually after the fifteenth of the month. Also, sweet corn and the rest of the vegetables were planted. The garden was our food basket, so to speak. Sometimes Mother canned more than 200 quarts of green beans. Also, many quarts of tomatoes and tomato juice were canned and placed in the cellar with the beans, kraut, and corn. We also canned several bushels of peaches every summer. The beauty of home-canned peaches is that they can be processed when they are ripe. A peach canned when it is ripe is filled with flavor and contains a special texture much tastier than those processed when they are still half green.

At the same time the garden was being prepared and planted, so were the cornfields. The soil first had to be turned with a breaking plow. This tool was pulled by our team. It turned a twelve-inch furrow. It took a long time to plow a field with two horses. The process usually began very early in the spring, no later than early March. Dad always felt it was best for the turned soil to freeze a time or two before he began the second and third processes, dragging and discing. Sometimes the field would be dragged twice, before discing and a second time just before planting the seed in the ground. Our soil was not sandy, and thus it was resistant to all forms of preparation for planting. I can still see that little horse-drawn disc bouncing around like a rubber ball over some very large clods of clay soil. Yet, Dad would stay with it until the soil fell apart, and a workable seedbed was established. He did, however, talk a lot about how uncooperative the soil was.

Corn planting was a taxing operation. For a productive result, the seedbed had to be well prepared to receive the seed. The weather needed to cooperate too. The planter had to be in good working condition. It was important that the fertilizer containers and the containers that held the seed corn be free from rust and function properly . The fertilizer and seed systems were both driven by chains. As the planter rolled along, the wheels of the planter drove the chains that caused a pre-set amount of fertilizer to drop into the tubes running to the metal shoes that were piercing the soil. The seed corn followed the same path. All went well unless one or both of the shoes became plugged with mud. This could happen as the planter was driven through wet soil. In those days there were no electronic devices that warned the driver of the malfunctioning units. One could go quite a ways before the problem was discovered, then the driver had to do two things. First, it was important to clear the mud that was blocking the seed and fertilizer. Second, the one driving the machine needed to go back from whence he (on this farm all who worked the fields were male) had come and dig down in the furrow to see where the plug occurred. Sometimes it was impossible to see where the planting process had stopped. But usually it occurred when the machine was pulled through a low place. Our land was rolling, which means high areas and low. Sometimes it was only after the rest of the plants came up that one could see just where replanting had to be done. And that was the work of our job planter.

The job planter carried seed corn only. It had two handles. The operator would pull the two handles apart. The corn would fall down a chute and be stopped by two metal plates held tightly together by pressure from the handles. The plates would then be jabbed into the soil and the handles pushed together to let the grain out. Then the process would start over. If one could strike a steady rhythm, a lot of corn could be replanted in a short period of time. Of course, this corn always matured later and sometimes did not do well at all.

But I am ahead of my story. Planting the corn required the driver of the horses to attempt straight lines across the field. Driving horses is much easier than driving cats, but horses also have minds of their own, so the driver had to remain alert. As the planter was driven across the field, a metal arm was extended to make a small furrow about two feet to the side of the planter. The driver would follow that furrow as he came back across the field. It was a way of keeping the spaces between the two rows laid down by the planter looking uniform across the field. On our farm it didn't matter what row of corn one chose, for our horse-drawn cultivator tilled only one row at a time. Later, when we moved to tractors with two-row cultivators, it was important to make sure one was in the two exact-spaced-rows laid down by the planter. A row did not need to be off much for the cultivators to cut down the stalks. Recently online I saw a thirty-six-row planter. Wow! How corn planters and corn planting have changed! Today many farmers use the no-till method. This approach prevents soil erosion but also requires chemicals to keep the weeds under control.

One year, Dad checked the corn as he planted it. This term means that the hills of corn were planted in such a way that they could be cultivated row by row and also crossways. This process eliminated hoeing. One could look down the way the field had been planted and see straight rows. One could also look across the field and note that those rows appeared straight as well. But to achieve this check required extra time and labor. It was not really efficient. The field looked nice, but the process must have been developed in the mind of some well-organized dreamer. Dad planted the corn this way one year, and then abandoned the method.

In the early years we hoed the corn. On our farm it was a family affair. Dad and we boys would each take a row and cut the weeds and loosen the soil around the corn roots. One had to be careful not to cut the corn itself. Usually the hoeing went quite expeditiously. But there was one end of a certain field that was infested with morning glories. These things climbed the stocks, wrapped their tentacles tightly around them, and choked them to death. So we had to cut the glories off at the ground then unwrap them from the corn stocks. It was time consuming. Thank heavens it was only one field and just a small part of that venue. As one who has sermonized a lot across the years, I find the morning glories a metaphor for life. There are some habits that can begin with a lovely bloom but ultimately so fully take over our lives that all joy is gradually chocked off. One year our Palmer Elementary School sold seeds as a fund-raiser. I do not know the purpose of that particular activity, but my box of seeds contained a packet of morning glory seeds. My dad said, "We don't want any of those things. They make life difficult."

There is one experience of hoeing corn that for me stands out above all the others. It was a hot summer day, and we were covering a large field with our hoes. J. Wallace Hamilton, a Methodist minister, once said of long rows he had to tend, "When I looked down those rows, I understood what the Bible meant when it used the term, 'From everlasting to everlasting.'" Well, on this hot afternoon, when we came to the end of the field after completing several trips across it, Dad said we should take a rest. He had stashed a jug of water near a spacious tree just over the fence in the pasture field. So we climbed over the fence and gathered under the tree. The water jug was passed around. We sat there and talked for quite a while until Dad alluded to a comic strip of the time. It showed where a farmer had spent so many hours resting under a tree that neither grass nor weeds remained. Dad suggested that we needed to get back to work before we killed all the grass. I felt something very important that day under the huge tree. I truly did belong to this family. We were a very close group, and I belonged. A great feeling for a young boy. A great feeling no matter one's age. And now as I reflect on that moment, that moment when we passed the water jug around, I realize that we were sharing a special kind of communion. Family Communion. Even now I remember and rejoice. How blessed we boys were to feel accepted and loved, to know we belonged to something bigger than ourselves. Thanks be to God.

In late summer some of the corn was cut and blown into the silo. Silage provided cattle a gastronomical treat that met many of their nutritional needs, especially when some ground grain and supplements were added. Our silo was only thirty feet high. I cannot remember its circumference, but it did hold quite a lot of the chopped corn. Silo filling, like thrashing in that day, was also a community affair. Several farmers would get together and help each other during silo-filling time. The process required a silo-filling machine (an ensilage cutter) to be set up near the silo. A pipe was run from the machine to the top of the silo. The machine was usually powered by a farm tractor. The blower had to turn at a high rate of speed to lift the chopped fodder up and over the edge. One man would gently guide the corn stalks as they moved toward the rapidly turning cutting blades. As the stalks approached the blades, they were held down tightly by two rigid metal rollers. Those rollers always presented a danger for the one feeding in the stalks.

One day while Walter Bingham, the man who owned the farm on which Uncle Tom and his family lived, was feeding the machine when one of his hands got caught in the rollers. He could have lost his hand, even his life. But he thought quickly. With his other hand he was able to grasp the lever that stopped the rollers. He then reversed them and freed his injured extremity. He was several weeks recuperating. Farming can be dangerous. One needs to be very careful. And that fact of long ago is still true.

I have known more than one farmer with missing fingers. One man on the Derby Methodist Church Circuit got an arm caught in a corn picker. He was near a state highway, but a row or two of corn stalks hid him from traffic. He was able with his free hand to break a stalk off, attach his red bandana to it, and when he heard a car coming, lift it up and move it around some. He did all of this with one hand. After several hours someone saw the handkerchief and stopped to investigate. He was rescued, but he lost his hand. I visited him a few days after this hair-raising event. He was indeed grateful that someone saw his plea for help. Farming often presents the worker with times of major danger.

Of course, today the whole process is totally different. Now the corn for the silo is processed with a machine that cuts and chops it right in the field and blows it into a special wagon. The corn is then taken to the silo and unloaded into a blower system that lifts it up and over the top and lets it drop into place. The whole process is a one-man operation. Two are probably better. And I am certain one still needs to be vigilant. Farmers often are working alone, and accidents are always waiting to happen.

The rest of the corn on our farm that was not used for sileage was cut and shocked. This task was accomplished by tying together four stalks of corn in a certain way to form a skeleton around which more stalks could be brought together. The person cutting the corn would go out several rows, maybe eight, from this form, cut the stocks while moving toward the waiting structure, and then place the newly cut stalks against the skeletal frame. This process continued until a full shock, about thirty-two stalks, was completed. Then a stalk or two of corn was wrapped around the top of the shock to secure the whole unit. The corn then stood in the field for a few weeks to dry.

Sometime after the shocked corn was dry enough, Dad would go to the field and begin to husk it. Often he would toss the ears of corn in a pile and leave them on the ground for later pickup. As a preschooler I always liked to go with Dad to retrieve those piles of corn. Our dog, Ole Prince, was always with us. He could smell a mouse a mile away. And often there was a mouse or two under the corn. The dog would usually dispatch these rodents quickly. I learned violence quite early in life. And I was usually disappointed if we did not find a rodent for the dog to execute.

Today most of the corn is processed right in the field. A sheller head is placed on a combine and driven through the field of corn. Four or more rows at a time are shelled, and the corn is conveyed into a wagon being pulled along by the big machine. The shelled corn is taken to a large grain bin and unloaded into an electrically powered auger system that lifts the corn into the bin. It is much easier than it used to be when the grain was moved with large scoop shovels. Even aluminum scoops didn't make the job joyous. Also, new shelled corn is often trucked directly to a commercial elevator.

Wheat thrashing was much like silo filling in those days. The grain would be cut, dropped onto a moving canvas, which conveyed it to a mechanism that automatically bound it in sheaves with twine, then kicked each sheaf onto a carrier. When there were enough sheaves gathered for a shock, the operator hit a pedal with his foot, and all the sheaves dropped in one place. We boys would come along, set a couple of sheaves together to form the center and then fill in around them until the shock was large enough. A shock contained at least twelve sheaves. A cap sheaf or two was placed on top to shed water when it rained. The wheat would dry there until time for thrashing.

When the big thrashing machine came into our community, several farmers joined together to help each other to get the work done. They came with their horses and wagons. Those who didn't bring wagons worked with those who did. They would go to the field, load the sheaves onto the wagons, bring them to where the thrasher was, and one by one unload those sheaves on the feeder table of the separator. The wheat and straw would be separated inside the big machine, the straw blown onto a stack or fed into a baler that turned it into large oblong blocks of straw. The wheat was sacked and carried to grain bins. I remember one time when the thrashing machine was placed close enough to the grain bin that the wheat was deposited directly there. No bagging. No carrying. As I grew older I sometimes helped with the bagging of the grain. It was quite a day. And, as at silo-filling time, there was always a special meal for the workers to enjoy.

It was at one of those meals that I observed a neighbor's strange eating process. He would take a fork full of food, slowly lift it toward his mouth, and when the fork got within a foot of his face, he very quickly rushed it—almost jerked it—to his mouth as if he thought the food was going to get away. I was so fascinated by this process that I know now I watched too long. Even all these years later I can see the room, the radio, his chair, and the herky-jerky lifting of his food toward his mouth. He's been dead for more than fifty years, and the house was razed long ago. Memory! What a wonderful gift. If the long-ago scenes are positive.

The thrashing years I remember most were when a man whose name was Anthony Huck brought his large separator to serve the community. It was powered by a McCormick Deering commercial tractor. That outfit could separate a lot of wheat from the straw in a short period of time. And, of course, today the process of thrashing is totally different. The air-conditioned, self-propelled combine driven by one person will enter the field, separate the wheat from the straw, convey the wheat to a grain wagon. When the wagon is full, it will be taken to a storage grain bin and unloaded mechanically. Or the grain may be put on a truck and hauled to an elevator. No more shoveling. A couple of persons can do the work that took a dozen when I was a kid.

The haying seasons were another distinct summertime task. On this farm we raised clover, timothy, and alfalfa. I use the word seasons because the hay was cut at least twice. It was during hay season that I was given my first job that required some major responsibility. In those days hay on our farm was cut with a horse-drawn mowing machine. Once the hay had dried some, the next step was to gather it into manageable bunches with a dump rake. (Recently I saw a short clip from *The Wizard of Oz*. It showed a dump rake just like the one we had on that farm.) Mowed and cured hay was dragged for a distance, and when there was enough gathered in the rake, the operator would hit a foot pedal and leave a pile of hay behind. Once the hay was pulled into bunches, it was placed on the wagon with pitchforks. Our neighbor Raymond Reed owned a hay loader that was pulled behind the wagon and lifted the hay onto it mechanically. Mr. Reed had no children. Dad had four sons. We were his hay loaders. Also, to use a hay-loader, one had to gather the hay together in a windrow. That required a side delivery rake. Later, on another farm, we had the proper rake as well as a hay baler.

Sometimes the hay was shocked, that is, stacked up into mounds about four or five feet high and a few feet across. Either way, the hay would finally be loaded onto the wagon and brought to the barn. One of my early jobs was to make sure that the hay was loaded in such a manner that it didn't fall off the conveyance. Only once do I recall such a catastrophe. We lost part of a load on the way to the barn. We had to stop and reload.

Of course once we made it to the barn, the hay then had to be unloaded. This task was accomplished by using a hay fork, which was shoved down through the hay, handles pulled to set the hook. Then a horse would, through rope and pulley process, lift it from the wagon and up to a track in the top of the barn. When the load reached the track, it would move high above the mow until it reached the spot where Dad wanted to drop it. At that point he would yell "Stop!" as he pulled the trip rope. The hay would fall in place, and the horse would stop.

My job early on was to ride the horse. Dad usually placed a board at a spot beyond which the horse should, under no circumstances, be allowed to go. But I always heard him yell and stopped before I ran the hay fork off its rail. Dick did this task before I took over. Sometimes we were in competition for it. Oh, yes, the Hill boys thought work was just great. We wanted to be useful. Being a contributor to the task meant we were needed. We belonged on the team. And belonging always felt good.

It was important to get the hay into the mow at a time when it was dry enough but not too dry. One time Dad pushed the process a bit too fast. The hay was not cured enough. It began to heat more than normal. Dad thought there was a chance of spontaneous combustion, meaning that the hay might ignite and burn the barn down. It could have happened. He was so concerned that he walked across the mow to inspect it more closely. It did not explode. Some of the hay on which he walked, however, rotted. That was a small thing. He was a bit more careful after that.

Sometime before the United States entered into the Second World War, we transitioned from horse power to tractor power. Dad bought a John Deere H, a small tractor. Dad seemed to fear purchasing a larger unit. This little tractor pulled one turning plow. Yet, that was all the horses could pull, and they had to rest from time to time. The tractor did not need rest.

I do remember that when the tractor was delivered, it was put in the barn until after the local election. Dad was a township trustee, and he didn't want anyone to think that he was making money. So we hid the tractor. He lost the election anyway. He lost because he tried to change one practice that catered to a particular family in the community. Some things can't be changed if you want to keep a political job. It is important to know to whom the gravy goes.

In later years I knew a former township trustee in Gallia County. He told me that the trustees with whom he had served in former years wanted to trade graders every three years. "We didn't need a new grader that often," he opined, "but the other boys were getting a 'kick-back,' and they wanted to trade as often as possible," he said.

There was a fall evening, which I remember very well, when Dad was serving as a township trustee. A car drove up the lane and parked near the garage. I think Dad stepped out onto the back porch to check to see who was approaching. For quite a while we heard him talking with someone. Finally, Dad said something like, "I'll check on that first thing in the morning." When he came back in, he told us that the visitor was a person whom we all knew. The man's wife had left him and the family. The youngest child, a boy, was about my age. There were two older children. This father was struggling with how best to care for the children. He had decided, at least for the moment, to see if the youngest son could be placed in the Washington County Children's Home. He had come to Dad for help. The next morning Dad made the call, and the home received the boy. Later, the Marietta Times carried a story with a picture of the lad sitting in a soap box car he had made. He raced it in the Akron Soap Box Derby. I am sure his father brought him home as soon as he could.

There is one memory of the John Deere H I will share. Dad was opening a field—meaning, he intended to begin in the middle, turn a furrow one way, and then come back across and turn one up against the first. He would then simply move back and forth across the field, turning furrow after furrow. He wanted those first furrows somewhat straight. So at the edge of the field, he started the tractor, pointed it in the direction he wanted, had the engine running at a moderately elevated rate, lowered the turning plow to the proper depth, put the tractor in low gear, and put me on the driver's seat. The tractor had a hand clutch. He told me that he was going to walk to an elevated spot in the field that lay ahead. "When I reach that spot," he said, "I will wave to you. Push the clutch in and drive straight toward me." When I saw him wave his hands, I did as he told me. Slowly the tractor moved across the field and to the point where he stood. He stepped onto the tractor and took it from there. I felt like a king. I was working. I most always enjoyed work, especially if I could see the furrow I had turned. That did not always happen in ministry. In ministry one can do a lot of work but may never know whether a person has been helped or not.

Now before moving on, I want to share something of the economic situation into which I was born. Dad had worked the oil fields of Kansas and Oklahoma for about ten years. He became tired of working twelve-hour shifts six days a week. So he came back east and purchased a one-hundred-acre farm. He paid cash for it. Six thousand dollars. That was in the spring of 1929. Now if the reader knows American history, she is aware that the Great Depression hit in late October of that year. Ultimately, eggs were eleven cents per dozen, and many people didn't have the eleven cents. Dad purchased a bull (Grandmother Hill would have called the animal a man cow) for breeding purposes and borrowed twenty-five-dollars from the Beverly Citizens Bank for the purchase. Not long ago I gave a waitress that much as a gratuity. There were more than two of us dining.

There is a true story told that Mom and Dad needed some sugar and a few other staples that could be secured only at a store. So they gathered every cent that could be found in the house, and the total was less than three dollars. As I recall it, the total was two dollars and thirty-four cents. They went to Laymen where there was a crossroads country store run by Burt Goddard. They purchased what they needed and came home. How far would that small amount of money go today? No, it wouldn't even purchase a cheeseburger.

In later years, when I was serving the Yellow Springs United Methodist Church, I met a man who had been in that store many times when he was young. When I visited him from time to time, I would greet him with, "Let's go over to Burt Goddard's store and get an ice-cream cone." We would both laugh and together remember. That store has been gone for a very long time. It was once upon a time a landmark. That man's name was Guy Varner. His wife was Ruth.

One day my brother Bill went with our neighbor Raymond Reed to the stock sale in Marietta. At one time there were two of these sales each week, Tuesday and Thursday. On this day I suppose Mr. Reed took a steer or some animal to sell. When the sale was over, at least for the neighbor, he went to a restaurant for something to eat. Mr. Reed ordered a cheese sandwich and a glass of beer. When it came, the total for his lunch was fifteen cents. Mr. Reed looked at his bill and said, "My G--, fifteen cents for a cheese sandwich and a little glass of beer." I assume my brother also had something to eat. Mother probably gave him a little money for that. He never shared what he had, or its cost.

PART THREE
THE LARGER COMMUNITY

CHAPTER 6

THE M.E. CHURCH

AS I HAVE STATED BEFORE, my family was the first community I knew. And a great family it was. Not perfect by a long shot, but it was caring and nurturing. Mom, Dad, and my three brothers welcomed me, encouraged me, and helped me to grow and learn how to be part of the team. I am forever grateful for a wonderful beginning in the family that lived on a one-hundred-acre farm in southeastern Ohio. Oh yes, there were fights among us boys from time to time. I remember Bob and Bill in their early teens having a real physical knock down drag out confrontation in our upstairs bedroom one night. I have no idea what the problem was. Mother came aggressively up the stairs and stopped the fight. After she had calmed the gladiators, she said to them, "One day you boys will be miles apart and would give anything just to see each other, but then it won't be possible." She was so prophetic. In a few years Bob would be in France, and Bill and the rest of us would have given anything to see him once again. I, too, could whine from time to time; but looking back, I see that our home was stable. Mom and Dad were consistent in their parenting. We knew what to expect in relationship to our behavior. We always had good food and plenty of it. Few snacks. Most of the food was raised on the farm. We had clean clothes to wear, we knew we belonged, we had assigned work to do, and most of the time we felt super positive about who we were.

Yet, we are all aware that one cannot live long before other communities become important forces in life as well. And for me the first community beyond the family was the Palmer Methodist Episcopal Church. It was a small membership congregation that I remember with real appreciation and gratitude. And when I say "small," that word describes the number of folks who came each Sunday. A few years ago I met one of the present members of Palmer United Methodist Church. We shared some of the history of that congregation, and she allowed me to borrow and copy any part or all of the historic Sunday School Secretary's Book. I copied records for July 1938 through April 1945. I include below the minutes of one Sunday.

April 20, 1941

Sunday School opened singing "Face to Face." Prayer by Superintendent Austin Hill. Song, "In the Service of the King." Reading of the scripture lesson. Class No. 1. Teacher, Austin Hill Att. 15. Offering 31 cents. Class No. 2. Teacher Tom Beckner. Att. 7. Offering 10 cents. Total attendance 22. Total offering 41cents. Balance in treasury 83 cents.

This must not have been a really good day. Some days there were four classes.

My Aunt Helen was a teacher and so was Mother. In fact, the above minutes were written by Mother. Lizzie Hale was the official secretary. She must have been absent that April Sunday. A rare day. The Hales and Reeds were major workers in the church. In fact, it was Sally Hale, granddaughter of Lizzie and Lemuel, who met me at the church and lent the record books. In fact, she has helped me with some Palmer and Washington County historical information. To her I am grateful.

Jessie Murdock was my first Sunday School teacher at Palmer M. E. She was special. She made me feel like I belonged in this larger world. She talked about Jesus in such tones that I knew when I met him, I, too, would like him. I remember picture cards depicting important religious stories. These were given out every Sunday. One of the pictures stands out in my mind even now. It depicted the story of the huge cluster of grapes that Caleb and others brought back from their reconnaissance trip to check out the Land of Canaan. "And they …cut down a branch with a single cluster of grapes, and they carried it on a pole between two men" (Numbers 13:23). The rest of that story tells of the nay-sayers, who opposed going on over into the land and securing it for themselves. Caleb wanted to go, but the majority said "No." So the Children of Israel wandered forty years in the wilderness. The point of the story is this: If we fully trust the Power of the Universe, we can do more than we may think. We don't have to stay in the wilderness of life forever.

I will never know just how those cards and Mrs. Murdock's stories from those cards affected my life. Thanks be to God for those lay people who give of their time and model the story of Jesus to little children.

One of my first freeze-framed moments from Palmer M. E. is a mental picture I carry from the first Children's Day Program in which I participated. In this mind imprint there is a group of children standing in the chancel, practicing a song that we sang the next day, which was Children's Day. The song was "Jesus Wants Me for a Sunbeam." I probably had no idea what I was singing about, but it felt good to be a part of that group. To belong is much of what life for me has been about. Yes, I have mentioned that fact before, but it is true.

There was a banjo clock on the north wall of the Palmer M. E. sanctuary. As a child, I used to watch its big hand slowly move as the preacher spoke. I remember Rev. Allen above all others. He came at 10:30. The church was on a circuit, so he held services for two rural congregations each Sunday morning. He started the service each Lord's Day immediately upon arrival and began to deliver the sermon at 11:00. He felt compelled, I suppose, to give us our money's worth, so he held forth for one solid hour. Some days I thought the big hand would never get around to the "Amen" part. I spoke at that church a couple years ago. I asked about the clock. Sally Hale told me thieves had broken in and stolen it. It seems that nothing is sacred anymore. Maybe never was.

I also remember sitting on the front seat in that little sanctuary with my brother Dick one Sunday morning. We were singing, and I must have been overdoing that joyous work loudly in the ears of my brother. Dick turned to me and told me to quiet down. Mom and Dad were seated directly behind us, and Mom said, "Let him sing." So I continued, in loud form, I am sure.

Because the pastor served six small membership churches, he was at Palmer M. E. every other Sunday. It was on one of the pastor's Sunday off that at close of Sunday School, just before the final song, someone suggested that Fletcher Reed share a letter the family had received from his sister, Mary Reed. Mr. Reed had already read the letter to the adult class, and some thought the children should hear it too. Mary was a missionary serving in India. I can still hear Mr. Reed's trembling voice as he read. Mary had been home on furlough. While in New York City, she had undergone a major health check-up. After returning to India, she received a report. Her letter told us that she had been diagnosed as having leprosy. This was not a major surprise, for she had been working with a leper colony for years. She stated in her letter that she would not be home again. "But," she wrote, "this frees me to move into the colony and minister to those whom I dearly love." She died in India and was buried there. A Methodist Church near Crooked Tree, Ohio, was named in her honor.

All the pastors of Palmer M. E. had some positive influence on our family. But one especially, mentioned above, exercised a major influence in my family's spiritual development. His full name was Ellsworth Abel Selah Allen. Mom and Dad were nominal church people, not yet fully committed to Christ. One Christmas, probably 1938, the pastor invited our family to share Christmas dinner with his family. When the meal was served, the pastor asked Dad to offer grace. Dad's response to the invitation was, "I don't feel worthy to do that." The good pastor and his wife were surprised. Later, as Mom and the pastor's wife were washing dishes, Mrs. Allen told my Mother something like, "Oh, Mrs. Hill, you need to give your life to Jesus."

It was probably in the spring of the following year that Uncle Carl Nutter, a kind of barn-burning evangelist, was booked to hold a revival meeting. The series of evening meetings created quite a stir in that rural community. The little church was nearly full every night. One night at the close of the sermon, when the altar call was given, I heard my mother say, "Austin, I am going." And she rose to her feet and started down the aisle. I was quite small, maybe five years of age, and was watching Mother go forward when I heard my Dad say to someone sitting beside us in the pew, "Will you watch my boy? I'm going with her." And he got up, moved up the north aisle, crossed from the left side of the sanctuary to the right, and knelt beside my mother. I could see he was weeping. That image is frozen in my mind forever. That night changed our family life a lot. We were in most ways already good people, responsible and hard working. This intentional move to become fully engaged with Christ and the Church just made life more fully focused on following the teachings of the One we call Lord. I don't think any of us arrived at perfection, but we kept reaching for it.

This event at Palmer M. E. moved the Hills from being nominal Christians to being committed believers. I can still see my family on a Sunday morning a few weeks after that revival meeting, kneeling at special benches surrounding the chancel. They were for that church the Chancel Rail. Mom and Dad are kneeling at those benches, so are Bob, Bill, Dick, and me. We all were made members of Palmer M. E. that morning. All of us may have strayed from time to time, but we always came back to affirm the Christian faith. A few years ago, when I first revisited that country sanctuary after a lifetime in ministry, I walked directly toward the chancel and knelt close to where I was kneeling when I was baptized that Sunday morning, scores of years before. It was as if time had stood still. I could feel my family members beside me as they were on that Sunday morning long ago.

In a few weeks following that special morning at the chancel, Dad became the Sunday School superintendent. Then he became the custodian. Of course, his services were voluntary. He also became a trustee and worked to improve the old building. So much of our life revolved around that church and the Christian faith. Too, grace was offered at every meal. And often there were evening Bible readings and prayers in our home.

As I look back on those early days of church, I realize that Dad and Mom were very conservative in their way of thinking. They brought with them to their newfound faith, beliefs that they were given in their youth. Faith for them rested on a lot of don'ts. It was sinful to play cards, attend movies, and dance. There was even discomfort with playing ball on Sunday. My faith understanding was, in some ways, controlled by that kind of thinking until I attended seminary and learned more fully the depths of God's grace as taught and lived out in the life of Jesus the Christ. Jesus taught that God loves all of us, in spite of the fact that we often are not so loveable. As a pastor who a few years ago served Hilliard United Methodist Church put it, "God loves us no matter what." The theologian Paul Tillich taught, "God has accepted you. All you need do is to embrace that acceptance." Once a person grasps the meaning of that statement, it will change their life.

After my brother Bob was killed in action November 19, 1944, in France, Mrs. Ella Mae Townsend, a woman we knew who lived in Waterford, recalled that Bob had confided to her, when he was home on furlough, that he had, for some time, experienced a recurring dream. He told her that in this dream, he was at a worship service in the Palmer M. E. Church and heard a great shout from outside. Someone announced that Jesus was coming. In his dream he was the first person out of the building. Second was Fletcher Reed and third was Lemuel Hale. I have been unable to confirm the sequence of all three deaths, but I do know that Lemuel Hale died in the spring of 1945, about five months after Bob was killed in the war.

My church experience was expanded by the Methodist Ladies Aid Society. This group of ladies met several times each year. They raised money for various mission projects. At one of their monthly meetings, when I was probably two or three, I went to the host's bedroom and was opening drawers and closing them. I closed a drawer on one of my fingers and hurt it. Of course, I cried like a baby. My mom came running to comfort me. The man of the house, who was present, said, "Now maybe he will keep his hands out of things." Mom was not happy with his remark.

The Ladies Aid held two major events every year, first, a New Year's Day Oyster Dinner, and second, the summer Ice Cream Social. I recall one New Year's Day Oyster Dinner in particular. It was held at Cecil and Annie Sheets' home, an old brick house that was quite lovely. The oyster soup was prepared upstairs as I remember it. And soup it was, for there were few oysters in it. I think one was fortunate if there were two oysters in the bowl, mostly one, I think. But there was laughter and fun.

The night before that dinner while Mother was helping prepare for the following day's festivities, some older boys were driving an old Model T Ford all over a hill side pasture field near the house. They were making quite a racket. They must have been the featured attraction for some of us for at least twenty minutes. When they came back down to earth, Mom discovered that my brother Bill was one of the passengers. She just about blew a fuse.

Mr. Joe Lawrence drove his new Studebaker four-door sedan to the dinner on that New Year's Day. When he was trying to leave, one of the rear wheels was sitting on a little patch of ice. He could not get the car to move. I can still see him spinning his wheels and moving the car back and forth, trying to extricate it from the ice trap. He was finally successful. I can still see that green Studebaker. And that has been nearly eighty years ago. I thought, "A new car, held hostage by a little piece of ice."

The other major event of the Ladies Aid was the Summer Ice Cream Social. This gathering was held at our house one year. The Beverly, Ohio, Ice Company, owned by Wayne Graham, according to Francis Sampson, a well-informed local historian, delivered a large amount of ice early in the day. After lunch the freezers were prepared. These freezers each held three gallons of mix and were turned by hand. I do not know how many people came to help, but the ice cream making was completed by late afternoon. It was then packed in such a manner to make it harden more. Then the wait, the long wait for me, began.

Sometime before the community folks began to arrive, the church women brought pies and cakes and spread them out on tables. Finally, the party began. I don't think I ever got enough ice cream. Maybe that is why even today I could eat that wonderful dessert three times a day and be ready for more. I don't know whether the Ladies Aid still functions or not. The church is still there. It is still functioning because a few faithful people keep the fires burning.

It was at one of those ice cream socials, held, I believe, at a house just off the southeast corner of the Square, where the Amos family lived, that those in charge of the social arranged for a Cakewalk. Each walker paid a dime to be in contention for the cake. The people walked in a circle much like playing Musical Chairs, except there were no chairs. One blindfolded person with a baton or broom stick in his hand stood near the circle, and at a particular moment, he lowered the stick in front of some lucky person who received the cake. I don't remember who won the cake, but I do remember that Mother was not pleased. Gambling! That is what it was, gambling! At a church event! And, of course, it was.

Maybe some of Mom and Dad's thinking has controlled my thoughts about the National Lottery. I have yet to buy a ticket. And the jackpot this week is around half a billion dollars. However, I don't think a dime for a chance on a cake will doom one to hell. I did once have a member who purchased a lottery ticket when the jackpot was in the high millions. She then worried that if she won, how it might devastate her life. I told her if she thought that was a problem, I would resign my appointment and handle her money for her. She didn't win. I don't know whether she was glad about the outcome or not.

The Methodist Episcopal Church has gone through several name changes since the late 1930's, when my family and I attended Palmer M. E. Until 1844, it was The Methodist Episcopal Church. In that year there was a regional split over slavery. The M. E. South and M. E. North replaced the former unified denomination. The Methodist Protestant Church had already broken away from the mother church in 1828 over the desire for congregational rule. My Grandfather Nutter was a minister in that branch of Methodism. (A friend reminded me recently that the M.P.s were first to ordain women. Good for them.) These three branches of the church reunited in 1939 to form The Methodist Church. To make that union happen, the church fathers capitulated to the southern racists and created the Central Jurisdiction. This unit covered the whole United States and beyond. It was where all people of color were placed. Yes, the new Methodist Church was totally segregated. The Central Jurisdiction was a church within a church.

In 1968, the merger of The Methodist Church and the United Brethren Church resulted in The United Methodist Church. The new denomination moved swiftly toward integration. Today the big issue is how we embrace or reject the LGBTQ community. It appears that we will fracture once again. It took nearly a hundred years to bridge the 1844 split over slavery. It may take just as long to overcome the present storm, which is well along the way toward shattering our unity once again.

There have been several upgrades in the Palmer Methodist Church building across the years, including a brick bulletin board outside, electric lighting, lowered ceiling, and bottled gas heating. I am sure the windows have been replaced and insulation probably blown in the walls. When I attended in my childhood, there was no electricity and no bulletin board. There were two potbellied stoves, one on the north side of the sanctuary and one on the south. I can still remember just how long those stoves took to begin heating that space. I remember because Dad opened the building and started the fires every winter Sunday morning. I can still see myself close to one of those stoves, slowly turning round and round to get my body warm on all sides.

My parents did not limit our church experience to the Palmer M. E. Church. Mom and Dad were members of a Saturday night prayer meeting group that met in homes. I don't remember ever meeting at our farm. The gatherings were always in Waterford and Beverly homes, because that is where all the other members lived. My parents also were members of the Muskingum Valley Camp Meeting Association. The camp meeting was held every summer at Beverly in a large tent. I believe it always occurred in August. The Association would contract with an evangelist from somewhere to come in and preach. It was something like Lillian Smith stated in her book *Killers of the Dream* (1949). She said something to the effect that, "The Evangelist came to town every spring and every fall. He passed out guilt for an hour each evening and then invited the people to come forward and be relieved of it."

One night during Camp Meeting, Mom and I had been uptown in Beverly. She was shopping for a few things. As we made our way toward the tent, down near the Muskingum River, there was a summer thunderstorm rapidly approaching. We hurried inside. The flaps were secured, but we found our way in. The storm hit, and the tent danced like a leaf in a mighty windstorm. The lights flickered but did not fail. The patriarch of the association, "Uncle" Dave Townsend, stood up and said, "Everything will be all right. So long as this pole stands, we are safe." And the center pole stood firm. It was well anchored and unmoved by the storm's fury. The big blow passed, and the worship service began.

As I reflect on that experience, I see therein a major truth, a metaphor of life. We are aware that everyone experiences life's storms sometime during their earthly journey. The storm may be disappointment, loss of a loved one, health problems, or some other malady. If we focus totally on the problem, we may be destroyed. But if we are held firm by faith in the One who promised, "I will never leave you nor forsake you," then we will, one way or another, weather the strongest winds this world can send our way. Life is uncertain, but by faith we are made strong.

There was a certain man who attended the camp meeting every year. He would sit down kind of behind the piano. I don't recall seeing him sing or participate much in the worship. He whittled a lot. He often made some object out of wood and gave it to a child. His name was Dan Slater. Recently while visiting the Oliver Tucker Museum at Beverly, Ohio, I saw some of his art. He was a genuine local artist, and I didn't know it until now. I remember him as a quiet man, pleasant in every way.

There was one soul who almost always attended the camp meeting. Often he would not make it until the final night. Usually when the altar call was given, he would go forward. Following his spiritual awaking experience, he would be asked to say a few words. His testimony was something as follows: "I am glad that God has set me free. You know if God had intended us to smoke, He would have put a smoke stack up our back. And if He had intended us to drink [meaning alcohol], He would have put a reservoir on our shoulder." I expect most of the folks who knew him kind of snickered as he spoke. Even Christians sometimes have our doubts. As I think of this episode of Camp Meeting, I am reminded of an old saw that tells of a man kneeling at the altar praying,

"O God, come and fill me," and a woman nearby praying, "Don't do it, Lord, he leaks."

I was sharing this camp meeting story one evening some years ago with my district superintendent, John Longsworth, and laughing about it. Dr. Longsworth didn't laugh; he may have smiled a bit, then said, "Charles, there must have been some part of him that was always trying to be a better person, seeking to move up to an improved way of living. He may not have been able to fully achieve that to which he was being called, but he kept trying. He had a vision of what might be." And of course, that is something we should all remember before we make light of a seeker who seems never fully to find that for which they are reaching. We should encourage them to keep trying. God's grace is infinite. We are accepted, no matter what. Too, if each of us is truthful, we also, on occasion, fail to be as faithful as we want to be.

So even the best of us always has room for improvement. The good Apostle Paul wrote that he wanted "to know Christ and the power of his resurrection" (Phil. 3:10). He then goes on to tell us that he hasn't arrived yet, but "presses on toward the goal" (v.14). To be honest, when I meet a person who has reached perfection in this life and knows it, I usually slip away quietly and wonder how one can be absolutely sure.

It was on a Sunday night many years ago that Mom, Dad, and I were in attendance at the Waterford, Ohio, storefront Nazarene Church. I suppose the sermon had been on sanctification, also known as "the second work of grace." Dad had gone forward, knelt at the mourner's bench, and was praying to be sanctified. He was there for quite a while. Finally, the minister's wife said, "Mr. Hill, just stand up and testify to the fact that God has sanctified you."

Dad's response was, "That would be like me telling you I have a twenty-dollar bill in my billfold when I know I don't." As far as I am concerned, common sense goes a long way in living the Christian life.

What does love require of us as we relate to the rest of humanity? Let's start there and ask for strength to truly care about what happens to others, to the ones who Dr. Tom Dooley described as "those who don't have it so good."

There are other memories I have of that camp meeting. The first one I remember attending was held at Dodge Park in Beverly. I must have been about ten years of age. The evangelist was Watt Walker. He was a Native American from Texas. Quite a preacher, as I remember. At least six feet tall. Booming voice. One night he preached a sermon predicated on the story of the Ten Virgins (Matt. 25:1f). He presented the gathering with an object lesson. There were ten women on the front row. Five had oil lamps with wicks turned up and flames producing lots of light. The other five had lamps with wicks turned down and their light dying. The story is that one group was ready to go to the wedding feast, but the others had to go search for more oil. While they were purchasing more oil, the bridegroom came. The five with lamps burning went into the celebration. The five not prepared were not allowed to join the festivities. They were too late. The door was shut. One sermonic application of the story is, that if we are not prepared when Jesus comes, we will be lost and left in darkness for all eternity.

Sometime during the sermon the evangelist got off track and began to speak about women's clothing. Suddenly he pointed at one of the women holding a lamp and said, "Sister, you could use a ruffle on the bottom of your dress." Of course, the woman was embarrassed. Probably petrified. Yes, angered, I am sure. And rightly so. If, however, that woman had an understanding of psychology, she might have said, "Reverend, you have just revealed more about yourself than you may have meant to."

When I was a student at Rio Grande College, now University of Rio Grande, the psychology professor stated one morning in her lecture, "All behavior has meaning. If your pastor preaches all the time on one issue, like drinking alcohol, then probably that is one of his problems." After hearing that statement, I was careful to check out what I was saying, and why I was saying it. The truth is, however, if we are truly observant, all behavior does have meaning, if we know how to read it.

The main forces behind the Muskingum Valley Camp Meeting Association were Harley Townsend and his Uncle Dave. They had built the platform and all the seats, provided the electrical equipment, and stored the same when not in use. Harley's son, Gail, told me recently that there were no written records of this group, but he had parts of a seat or two as icons of that once-upon-a-time very viable religious group. It was, I believe, the forerunner of The Waterford Nazarene Church.

My family and I visited a number of religious services that were held in our part of Washington County. One summer a tent was pitched at the corner of our township road and State Route 339. The preacher in charge was a man whose last name was Mayle. One night the sermon was a real barnburner. I was very young, but I remember a story he told about a beautiful young woman who was the "belle of the ball." She had been under conviction for some time . On this one night the church folks pleaded with her to repent of her sins and give her life to Christ. She refused to make that leap of faith. Within a few days she came down with spinal meningitis and died. The preacher drew a word picture of the horrors of her death, and how she was now suffering in hell for all eternity." I have a feeling that I did not sleep well that night. In fact, there were many nights when the sermons were more of a load than a lift.

Another preacher came to the community and held services not far from where the Truman Wells' Farm was located. I believe the building had been a one-room school. The evangelist went by the name of Sister Nuby. She was really an exciting speaker. Each night before she began her sermon, she knelt at the altar and sang:

> If I have wounded any soul today,
> If I have walked in my own willful way,

THE M.E. CHURCH

> If I have caused one foot to go astray,
> Dear Lord, forgive.

She told a story about visiting Father Divine's Heaven in New York City. He was a man on a mission. He was widely known in the first decades of the twentieth century. He founded the International Peace Mission. Some see him as the first civil rights leader. From what I have read, he did a lot of good. He threw great banquets where the finest food was served to hundreds of people at no cost to those attending. Many of these guests were poor. However, some people saw him as a charlatan. He did present himself, according to some reports, as the reincarnation of Jesus Christ. Sister told us that as she entered the complex, she was met at the entrance by one of his special devotees. "As I opened the door to Father Divine's study," she said, "this young woman suddenly fell backward and let out a great sigh. 'Oh, did you feel that overpowering spirit of Father hit you as we stepped in here?'" Sister Nuby, in a very condescending manner, said she told her, "I didn't feel anything at all." Sister was quite a performer, preacher, and entertainer.

CHAPTER 7

THE PALMER ELEMENTARY SCHOOL

THE SECOND COMMUNITY that had a major part in helping to nurture my young life was the Palmer Elementary School. It had two classrooms and one smaller room which was used as the music room. The music room was also used to prepare food for all eight grades after the beginning of World War II. When the war began, the government discovered that many of the recruits were malnourished. So, to remedy that problem, a school lunch program was developed and supported by the New Deal Administration. I still have the dish I used for those lunches. There was a folding door wall between the two classrooms. These doors were opened from time to time when there was a PTA meeting or a special program in which all eight grades participated.

There were no restrooms or running water. There were two outhouses, one for the boys and one for the girls. The boys' unit was a four-seater. I assume the girls' unit was the same. There was an outside pump from which we could get water to drink. On very cold days the boys sometimes put water on the concrete near the pump, let it freeze, then skated on it. As I remember, the teachers were not too keen on our skating, nor were our parents. Such activity was hard on shoes. Shoes cost money. And there was very little money in those days.

In those early days at Palmer Elementary, we were encouraged to wash our hands before eating lunch. Because there was no running water in the building, a pail was filled at the pump then placed in the cloak room along with a wash pan, soap, and towels. Most of us took advantage of that arrangement. Probably because our mothers told us to do it.

Also, in that pump area, when the weather was warm, girls would, with chalk, mark off blocks on the concrete and play Hopscotch. I never understood how the game worked. I do know the girls tossed an object into a specific block, then hopped on one foot to retrieve it, and hopped back. I never tried it. I know Google would tell me all about that game if I asked. I'm not asking.

But I am getting ahead of my story. The year before I entered the first grade, my cousin Mary Beckner, who had been in school for a couple of years, invited me to come as her guest for a day. She guided me through my first school experience. I clearly remember the Porter twins. They were in third or fourth grade. Beautiful girls. They made over me and I fell in love with them. I just knew I would marry one of them, maybe both. But those fantasies soon flew away. One of those girls died of tuberculosis before she ever reached adulthood. I don't remember much else that happened that day. Just those two beautiful girls. Had my family included a sister, I might have felt differently. Who knows?

It must have been later that year—the last day of school— and some of the classes were celebrating with a wiener roast on the Bingham farm, where the Beckners lived. Aunt Helen suggested to Mom that I join the group to further prepare myself for the coming fall, when I would be a first-grade student. I don't remember a lot about the activities of the day. There was a wiener roast. And there was an older girl, maybe an eighth grader, who was there. She was beautiful (is there a pattern here?) and she played guitar. I still remember one of the songs she shared. The chorus:

> Bury me beneath the willow,
> 'Neath the weeping willow tree;
> And when he knows that I am sleeping,
> Maybe then he'll think of me.

I liked school more than some did. It was a place where I made friends and learned to read, write, and do arithmetic. It is hard for me to remember today, but my writing education began with number two lead pencils, and then in the second grade we moved to metal tipped pens—the kind that had to be dipped in ink each time a word was written. We learned to print in first grade but were soon moved into cursive writing. My grades were, maybe, a bit above average. No one, however, would define me as a brilliant student. Sarah Jane Stollar Bolinger, who entered first grade with me, recently suggested in a letter that Chester Love and I were a bit more gifted than others. Truth is, I tried to keep up with Chester, but he was always ahead of me scholastically. I did take plenty of time with social contacts as well as daydreaming.

That first year of school presented me with a major challenge. I became quite ill. To my knowledge the problem was never fully diagnosed. I was put to bed for three weeks in the front bedroom where I was born. It was near Christmas and the weather was cold. A fire was kept burning in the fireplace. The only clear memory of that time is that I learned to read. My book was the Bible, the first few chapters of Genesis. When I returned to school, I soon caught up with the rest of the class and then moved on to second grade at year's end.

It must have been at Christmastime in my second year of school that I was able to print coherent simple sentences. As Christmas approached and my mind led me in a number of ways, I decided to write a letter to Santa. I can still remember that letter, kind of messy and unattractive. I am sure there were smudged areas and probably some food marks on it. But in it I told Santa exactly what I wanted him to bring me. I took the letter into the fireplace in that front bedroom where I had lain sick for so long the year before. Now there was no fire, but the flue was open. I held the letter close to the chimney and let go. It actually floated up the chimney. I knew Santa would get it. Sometimes we do let our children live in a fantasy land, but sooner or later we have to get real.

My older brother Dick told me the truth about Santa. I was furious and said, "But the Easter Bunny is real." Dick said, "No, he, too, is our mom and dad." I was furious. I did, however, soon get over it and move on. Later I misled my own children for a while. One Christmas Eve our third daughter squeezed in between our upright piano and the wall. There she watched Betty and me preparing the gifts. When we left the room, she ran upstairs and told her sisters, "I know who Santa is. It's Mom and Dad."

My first-grade teacher was Miss Margret Goddard. She was a very kind and helpful instructor. On occasion she would let us first graders go out and play at times other than recess. That would have been when the weather was inviting. Some years ago she sent to me some pictures of those early days. I am very grateful for the gift. She married after my first year and left our school. She was followed by Miss Wilma Nieb, who was still teaching when my family and I moved away.

There are many memories from those early days at Palmer Elementary. One of our learning centers was a sand box in the back of the first through fourth grade room. One year our teacher purchased beautiful white sand for the box. We thought it was wonderful. The sandbox was used to create country scenes and more. I clearly remember one Thanksgiving scene. There were pilgrims, dressed in black and white clothing. The men carried guns. The children looked like little adults. And I suppose there must have been a Native American or two in the mix, but we would have called them Indians. No, kids, there were neither computers nor cell phones, neither projectors nor electronics of any kind. We had lots of fun, but you would find school with such limited equipment dull, dull, dull.

Our music teacher, Miss Bonnie Bingham, came once a week for maybe thirty or forty minutes. We would sing. She always brought with her a windup record player. She would play some music and invite us to sing along. I was always eager to have Miss Bingham come. Music, for me, was great fun. It wasn't Miss Bingham who gave me piano lessons in the music room, but the teacher who followed her (Miss Bingham had married and moved on). I was not a good music student. I didn't practice. Oh, how I regret not learning to play that beautiful instrument. As it has been said, "Smart I got too late."

There is one activity I remember as if it were yesterday. I was in the fourth grade at the time. Miss Wilma Nieb, who was a wonderful teacher, had instructed the class to write a short story that we would read to everyone. I think it was to be just a paragraph or two. One by one we went forward. I read my story and sat down. I probably wondered whether I had done well or not. Insecurity was usually my closest companion. Melvin B. followed me. He moved to the place where we had been instructed to stand and began to read. I thought he was doing very well, certainly better that I had done. Then Miss Nieb stopped him. "Melvin," she said, "may I see your paper?" There wasn't a mark on it. He was, as they say, "making it up as he went." I doubt that he received a very high grade. But I thought he was doing very well. I wish she would have let him finish. That was a piece of some really creative writing.

It may have been when I was in second grade, one family in the school was reported to have head lice. Mom and Aunt Helen must have gotten their heads together and decided they did not want us staying at the school if that family of lice-laden-kids came. They came. And I can still see the Beckner and Hill kids moving through a gap in the woven wire fence that enclosed the east side of the playground. I see them heading across the fields toward home. I don't know what all happened, but we were in school the next day. We were spared the rod and the lice.

At the time when I was probably in the third grade, we were told that the school playground was about to receive a new addition. And a welcome addition it was. Teeter Totters. Seesaws. Oh, I know, no one would be excited about such a mundane thing today, I suppose. But back then they were a wonderful gift. We stood in line just for a turn on one. Half of Teeter Totters and Seesaws were low enough for the first and second graders, and the others higher for us big kids. They were made in farm shop at Waterford High School and installed by the makers. What a gift.

Outdoor activity at Palmer Elementary consisted of playing games of various kinds. For many of us boys, playing softball in the fall and spring was fully embraced. On occasion the softball team played other grade school teams. That was always great fun. Also, in good warm weather we took our lunch pails and sat under a tree as we visited and consumed our peanut butter, jelly, bologna, or egg sandwiches. There was a row of trees along the west side of the school grounds that made inviting places to gather at noon. Too, I have already mentioned hopscotch for many of the schoolgirls. In winter when there was snow on the ground, we played Fox and Geese. Also, forts were constructed by rolling snow up into chunks that could be stacked to enclose a bit of space. We then threw snowballs at each other. A few times we became Eskimos and built igloos. We would return to class with wet clothes and by evening have runny noses.

The last day of school in May of 1944 was unusual. When I entered the school building that morning, I sensed that something was wrong. I could feel it in the air. It was kind of like a dog hearing distant thunder and being stressed. The atmosphere of that classroom kind of intimidated me. It was evident that Mrs. Fisher, the teacher for grades five through eight, was not happy. We soon discovered the problem: a group of eighth grade boys had boarded the bus taking high school students to Waterford.

These boys were going to have a special free day on the town and celebrate the ending of the school year. Mrs. Fisher was having none of it. She went home (no phone at the school) and called Mr. W.F. Hughes, the superintendent of Waterford High School. He met the bus and sent the boys back to Palmer. When they entered the building, Mrs. Fisher was waiting for them.

She had asked some of us to go out to the brush pile, which had been prepared for our last-day-of-school wiener roast, and bring in some branches. She told us how many. As the boys entered the classroom, she became very red in the face and said, "I had planned to talk with you about why you did this, but I am not going to do that. Line up." And she took the branches that were quite strong and literally decimated one on each of the boys. It was a frightening experience for all of us who were in the room. I was seated near the front where pieces of wood were flying around like autumn leaves driven by a stiff wind. Later the boys were not very eager to join the fun, games, and wiener roast. Mrs. Fisher said something like, "Come on now and enjoy the fun and food. What was, was, but now it is over. Let's forget it. Come join the fun." As the reader can see, after more than seventy-five years I still remember the event quite clearly. Some images once etched on the memory panel of the mind fade very slowly, and some never totally dissolve.

My best friend in Palmer Elementary arrived on the scene when I was in the third grade. Chester Love was his name. His dad was a pilot. Not a commercial pilot. Small planes. He owned a little Taylor Craft two passenger. He flew fire patrol over southern Ohio. Chester (also in the same grade) and I were competitors in school and fast friends when we were not in class. Chester would steal cigarettes from his mother, and we would smoke them. Camels. We were pretty young for such activity, but we were on a fast track. On a rainy Sunday or two, I remember going up to his bedroom, cracking the window, and smoking cigarettes. We blew our smoke out the window. I don't think we inhaled the smoke, just like President Clinton. We also read comic books. Chester had hundreds of them.

Chester and I were quite capable of creating exciting activities. One day Chester took some of his mother's cigarettes, and we went out to the hog house. It had a loft where there was a host of sparrows. We found some sticks or boards and used them to kill birds. Now and then we stopped to smoke. That behavior kind of indicates that we could have grown up to be killers. I just don't know why we engaged in such brutal behavior. Maybe we should have asked ourselves why we enjoyed killing those birds.

One Sunday afternoon we rode our bicycles around the area and smoked. I arrived home a bit late. Mom, Dad, and the family were going to a camp meeting over near Sharpsburg, so I was informed. We ate quickly. I became very ill. I lost my supper. Later I diagnosed myself as suffering from nicotine poisoning. After emptying my stomach, I felt fine.

One Sunday afternoon when no one was at home, Chester and I got two guns out and did some shooting. I remember a rifle and a revolver. And how old were we? Maybe ten. Thank God we did not hurt ourselves or a horse or cow. Later, Chester moved to Kansas, and we lost contact until 1998 when Betty, my wife, and I stopped in Bakersfield, California, and met him and his wife for breakfast. We visited a few times after that.

On one visit in Springfield, Ohio, Chester's mother, Margaret, said to me, "Do you know that your dad sat up with my dad the night my father died?" I did. People did those kinds of neighborly things back then in the 1930s and 40s in southern Ohio. Back in those rural Palmer days, we knew each other, attended church together, worked together, and cared deeply about each other's welfare. We knew who could be trusted and who could not. Most everyone in our community was super trustworthy. Neighbors sat at night with extremely ill folks so others in the house could get some rest. Dad sat with Margaret's dad and someone else who died. Mom suggested people would not want him to sit with their loved ones, for when he was present, people died. Mom always looked on the bright side of events.

Chester and I could get into a lot of devilment for as young as we were. One time when he, his wife, and mother visited Betty and me in Springfield, Ohio, I reminded him of some of our behavior. One Halloween we were together. We walked up the road on the west side of the Square. Jim Murdock had left his ensilage cutter near the road. It was sitting in such a way that the two of us boys could roll it out and block half the state road. We did the deed. We moved on to the Ford boys' place. A farm wagon was sitting near the drive. Because of where it was stored on a slope, we were able to pull the block that was under one wheel and get it rolling. We moved it out across the state road into a field.

In one of our conversations, Chester told me that after I moved from the community, he and the Pugh boys, who lived down on Wolf Creek, were out one Halloween seeing what they could get into. They knew of a barn in which an ancient buggy was stored. They were able to get this vehicle out, jump in it, and ride down a major hill. One problem, they crashed at the bottom of the hill before they made it to the bridge. This valuable collector's item was shattered. Chester did not say whether the farmer ever knew what happened. Halloween pranks can get out of hand sometimes.

There was a Halloween story circulating in the Palmer community when I was a kid that received a lot of attention. Whether it was true or apocryphal, I cannot say. As it is told, a group of boys were out one Halloween and looking for some devilment to get engaged in. After some discussion they decided to take a farmer's buggy, disassemble it, take the parts to the roof of the barn, and reassemble them. So, they went to work. It took several hours to accomplish this deed; actually, most of the night. As they came down from the roof, worn out from all that work and, chuckling at their joyous achievement, the old farmer stepped out of the shadows, pointed his shot gun in their direction and said, "Great job boys, great. Now bring it back down." It is a good story, true or not.

It was while we lived in the Palmer community that my brother Bill was out with some teenagers on Halloween. They were taunting some poor soul out at Barlow, a small crossroads village. The victim started shooting at these kids. The girl, a teenager who was with my brother, discovered that she had been hit with a bullet. Her arm was bleeding. My brother, frightened half out of his wits, took her to Beverly and got Dr. W. D. Turner out of bed to save her life. Dr. Turner examined the girl, cared for the cut, but said that he could find no bullet in the arm. The bullet was not discovered until weeks or months later. One day the girl's mother put on the coat her daughter had been wearing on that scary October night, and the bullet fell out. The silk lining had kept the projectile from entering her arm yet allowed it to cut the skin. Saved by silk. Teenagers can be both fearless and a little insane at times.

Some years later, I too was in Barlow on a Halloween night. I don't know whether it was the same man or not. But there was an elderly man firing off a few rounds now and then. I heard one bullet zinging through the air, and it hit the ground not far from where I was lying in a ditch. As I said, youth often do not use good judgment.

Chester was graduated from the Colorado School of Mining and spent his life in the oil business. He spent five years in Saudi Arabia. Made a fortune, I expect. But he was still a very down-to-earth guy. Death overtook him a few years ago. He had lost his beloved wife to cancer and found this loss difficult to cope with. He came to Wichita, Kansas, for a visit with his aged mother. When she called him for breakfast, he did not respond to the summons. She found him still in bed, lifeless. He had died in his sleep. Margaret lived another year or two. She was in her nineties.

Chester's dad gave me my first plane ride. It was on a Sunday, late afternoon, towards the end of summer. Chester asked his dad if he would take me up. He agreed. I climbed into that little two-seater. Don manually pulled the propeller, and the engine came to life. He climbed in and taxied to the end of the field. He then turned the plane and headed directly east. The airstrip was in a pasture field. The strip had been graded to remove vegetation and bumps, but it was still very rough. The little plane shook, rattled, moaned, and groaned, but finally became airborne. I remember that we didn't miss some telephone wires by very much, but we made it. We flew over the south side of Palmer Square then on to the east side and looked down on our house and farm buildings. We flew over the church and school. A few minutes later we were back on the ground. When Mother heard what had happened, she was not very happy. She said, "You might have been killed." As I stated above, Mother's verbal expressions often reflected her super positive emotions about life's exciting moments. One statement I heard her say many times was, "I would be afraid to say that. I would be afraid God would strike me dead." As a child, about every time I did or said something that seemed wrong, I awaited the lightning bolt.

One memory of Palmer Elementary School had to have happened Tuesday, December 5, 1944. It was midmorning. A knock on the entranceway door suddenly caused everyone to lift their eyes from their schoolwork. When Mrs. Fisher opened the door, I could hear an exchange of words, but did not understand what was being said or who the intruder was. After a few moments, Mrs. Fisher stepped back into the room and said, "Wayne (that is my middle name by which I was known until young adulthood), you are excused to go with your brother." I wondered what this intrusion was all about. As we left the building, Bill told me that a telegram had arrived in the morning mail telling us that our brother Robert Warren had been killed in France. I was shocked and silent. I didn't cry. Just pondered what this tragedy meant to our family. I maintained that focus until I reached the back door of our house. I can still see myself resting my head on the framework of the back porch door and weeping. Our family's life was suddenly changed forever. Nothing would ever be the same again.

ROLLING HILLS

War causes so much pain to millions of good people. The scars it produces are never erased, even by the ever-moving tides of time. But Hitler and Japan had to be stopped. Bob and thousands of other young people gave their all to help sustain the freedoms that thinking Americans hold dear. I suppose that is one reason I am so disturbed with those who today call themselves Nazis and want to overthrow this democratic republic. Too many good people died for their sacrifice to be rebuked by young men and women who want instant gratification for their momentary whims. My revulsion also goes to those who would use their political power to thumb their noses at this democracy and embrace any lying tyrant.

CHAPTER 8

MEMBERS OF THE NEIGHBORHOOD

THE PALMER COMMUNITY was made up of a tight-knit group of common citizens. All were farmers. One or two may have moonlighted at something else, but their basic livelihood was secured by working the land. There was only one school and one church, so there wasn't much diversity. In other ways we were quite diverse. Church-wise, the Strauss family was Catholic. They drove to Beverly to attend Mass. Sometimes on our way to Palmer Methodist Church, we would meet them as they were coming home from worship. We didn't know much about the Catholic Church. In fact, I think we were a bit afraid of it. I know that one day when Mrs. Strauss was helping my mom prepare dinner for thrashers or silo fillers, she asked Mrs. Strauss why the Catholics pray to Mary. She told Mom that Mary, being the mother of Jesus, had control over her son. And a good son would do what his mother asked him to do. That is certainly one way to answer the question. The Strauss family were good people and excellent neighbors.

Our nearest neighbors were Raymond and Daisy Reed. I have mentioned them already. They were hard-working people and good neighbors. They had to be good neighbors, for before the Second World War began, the school bus turned around in their driveway. In winter the bus made some very deep cuts there. I never heard Daisy or Raymond complain about the driveway problem. The bus came down that little road to pick up just the Hill boys. Of course, beginning in 1942 with the onset of gasoline rationing, the bus no longer came down to pick us up. We had to walk a mile up to the main road to catch it. Raymond did not have good relational skills, but his wife Daisy was warm and friendly. She balanced everything out. I only remember seeing Raymond in church once. That was during the revival meeting in 1939. I suppose he received all he needed that evening. As far as I know, he never returned. It might have helped his vocabulary had he attended a few more times.

One summer morning I had gone over to check on the mail. The box was not far from the Reed driveway. I do not remember just what errand took me toward their house, but there in the driveway was a huge black snake. I must have yelled, because Daisy came running. She took a clothesline prop and nudged the black snake. It went slithering off into a building nearby. "Oh," she exclaimed, "there is another snake here." It was a small copperhead. She killed it. I then asked if she was going after the black snake. "No," she responded, "Raymond keeps black snakes in our buildings. They take care of the mice and rats." I decided to stay out of their buildings. Mrs. Reed told me that black snakes sometimes killed copperheads. I wondered about that. Just now I asked Google about this issue. It was stated there that "black snakes may eat other snakes, even copperheads." What I saw with my own eyes indicates that black snakes sometimes kill copperheads. I didn't see the copperhead being eaten. Maybe if Mrs. Reed and I had been more patient, we would have learned more. That is a thought to hold close.

One year I had some small part in a school play. It called for me to hum a tune at one point: "Home Sweet Home." I'd never heard of it. Mrs. Reed said she had it in a songbook. So one day she invited me over to her house. She took me into the parlor where her pump organ was located. She helped me learn the song, and I am sure I was a hit in the school play. Sometimes it's the little things that impress us. And sometimes we are more impressed with ourselves than the situation deserves.

Sometime about 1940, the Reeds purchased a very nice used Ford coupe. It may have been a 1938 or 1939 model. It looked like new. It was gray. Until then, wherever they went, the old Chevy truck was used for transportation. A Sunday or two after the purchase of their Ford coupe, Daisy (Mrs. Reed) asked me to ride with her over to Palmer Methodist Church. Raymond had the car pointed in the right direction. We got in, she started the engine, and we were on our way. She took off in second gear. She stayed in second gear up the east side of the Square, across the north side of the Square, and down the west side of the Square. When we got to the church she said, "I think I'll just park here close to the road ditch. Then when church is over I think I will just drive on around the Square. That way I will not have to turn the car around." And that is what we did. And in second gear.

I have already mentioned the Beckner family. Helen Beckner was one of my many aunts. Mother was one of seventeen children. Fifteen lived to adulthood, and all of them or their spouses had children. I have cousins I never knew. Aunt Helen and Uncle Tom were married in 1927. They had four children when they lived at Palmer: Howard, Delbert, Paul, and Mary. Douglass was born in 1944 after the family had moved from the farm. When all of us got together, we usually had a great time. My dad told me before he died that when he knew the Beckners were going to be our neighbors, he and Uncle Tom agreed that they would let the kids' disagreements stay with the kids. It worked. There was very little conflict among us. I do remember Mary telling me once that horsehairs, if put in water, would turn into horse-hair snakes. I never saw it happen. Just recently, however, I read that the same story was told in Europe regarding eels. Horsehairs could become eels if left in water for a certain period of time. That story, I think, originated in France. That information, too, is about as factual as most political commercials.

One time, Mom and I were going with Uncle Tom to Grandpa Nutter's house. Aunt Helen and Mary were in the front passenger seat of Uncle's big old Studebaker. Mom, Paul, Delbert, and I were in the back seat. When Uncle stopped to pay the toll on the Parkersburg Bridge, Delbert had covered himself up with enough bags of stuff that his body was hidden. I remember Uncle Tom saying to the toll taker, "Don't count too fast now, captain." Delbert got a free pass. Probably saved a nickel. Yet, a nickel in the 1930s was worth much more than it is today. We could purchase a good-sized candybar for five cents in those days, or a bottle of pop for the same amount.

After the Beckners moved from the Bingham farm, a family by the name of Williamson moved in. They didn't stay long, maybe a year or two. One story I remember Mr. Williamson telling was about being at a church service. A visiting quartet was singing. One song presented was "Will There be Any Stars in My Crown?" Williams said as three of the members sang the lyrics, the bass droned on in his deep voice, "No not one, no not one." He laughed heartily at his own joke.

The Payne family followed next. They, too, were good neighbors. It was still during the Second World War, and Dick and I would walk up to the Bingham farm, and the Payne kids would walk on with us to the bus house. (For the uninitiated, a bus house was a small shed in which we could avoid the rain, snow, and wind while waiting for the bus to arrive.) Billy was about my age, and Donna Jean was Dick's age. That walk was almost always pleasant. Of course, if it was raining or snowing, the joy of the walk was limited. One morning we were a bit early, and the Payne kids were just finishing their breakfast. Betty, their mother, had made corncakes. She invited us to have some. We did. That evening I was going on about how great those cakes were. Mother said something like, "I can make those cakes just as good as anyone else." She could, of course. She just never did it.

After we moved from the community, their son Billy attended revival services at Palmer M. E. Church and gave his life to Christ. He then invited his dad to come with him. Both became active Christians. Elmer became a self-taught local preacher. He was a dairy farmer. He had purchased the farm from Bingham. His workday before conversion began at 5:30 am. After his spiritual awakening and having a desire to preach, he had a lot to learn. He didn't know much about the Bible but knew he had to learn what he could. So he rose each morning at 4:30 a.m., started the coffee pot, and then read for about an hour. He learned. I heard him preach once at a little independent church near Veto. He was quite enthusiastic about the faith.

Jim Stollar lived on the northside of the Square. He and his son ran a farm together. They were not church folks, but Mrs. Stollar was a member of the Ladies Aid. I know that is fact because the Summer Ice Cream Social was held at the Stollar home one time. What I remember most about Jim is that he wore a large mustache and had a hearty laugh. Also, he repaired my toy wagon beautifully. The handle had broken at the point where it was attached to the steering mechanism. Dad and I took it up to Mr. Stollar in the car. He told me when he would have it ready. On that day I walked the mile or so to his house to retrieve it. He had repaired it perfectly. He even painted orange the newly applied straps of metal. I think the charge was fifty cents. Yet, it might have been a quarter. I pulled it home as if I were driving a new Mercedes.

Jim and his son Dan had the first pick-up hay baler in the community. It took three men to operate it: one to drive the tractor and two to punch and tie wires. Two men sat on wooden slats facing each other, one on each side of the baler. One man pushed wires through from his side, and the other received the wires on the other side. The latter twisted the wire ends together, thus securing the bale. As the next bale formed, it kicked out the tied bale. There was a block of wood one of the men had to drop in place to provide a path for the wires to be pushed in place. On an afternoon when it was nearly 100 degrees in the sun and dust from the process was raining down all over the pushers and tyers, it was not a job for the fainthearted. My brother Bill told me recently that he had, on a number of occasions, been one of the wire pushers or tyers. Also, that even though he had a handkerchief tied over his face, the dust was almost suffocating.

I saw the operation at least once. The men on the baler looked like they had been through a war. Of course, it wasn't long until we had self-tying balers. These balers used twine instead of wire. The first John Deere baler used wire for a while, but even that manufacturer soon went to twine. Later, on the second farm, our neighbor owned an Allis Chalmers baler that produced round bales. Some people thought that approach to processing hay would never catch on. Today I see round bales much larger than the neighbor's baler produced. I would call some of today's round bales "gigantic."

Down the road from the Stollar house lived the Cunninghams. This family also farmed for a living. Paris, however, the man of the house, also possessed construction skills. Our hillside barn, on the lower side, was in need of major foundational repair. The barn was sinking. Mr. Cunningham brought his railroad jacks, raised the barn up to level it, then built forms for new concrete support pillars. Dad and my brothers mixed the cement in a hand-cranked machine. The cement was then transferred from the mixer into the forms. After the cement cured sufficiently, Mr. Cunningham slowly let the barn down on the new piers. The repair was perfect. The barn stood until a few years ago when it burned. The origin of the fire, someone said, was an electrical short. I believe Mr. Cunningham helped to run cement in our cellar also. The cement on both jobs was mixed at the work location. I suppose there was ready-mix available, but we didn't use it. Wayne Cunningham, a son, played guitar. He gave my brother a lesson or two. Mrs. Cunningham was often upset with folks at the church. I don't recall the reason.

MEMBERS OF THE NEIGHBORHOOD

Near the Cunninghams lived Maude Murdoch. She was never married, so far as I know. She owned and operated a farm. I can remember her coming to church one morning driving a new Chevrolet coupe. That was probably in 1940 or '41. She probably came at other times as well. Her male friend for a period of time was a Mr. Orndoff. (He drove a green LaSalle. That car was manufactured from 1927 to 1940. It was considered a luxury automobile. Part of the Cadillac Division of General Motors.) Miss Murdock was a very well-respected person in our community. She was also physically attractive.

Across the road from the church was the Township Building. Mom and Dad voted there. We were there the night Dad lost his township trustee job. Someone on that porch said, "There's one who is gone." That man seemed to be happy at Dad's loss.

Dad was hurt emotionally because of the loss. But as my brother remembers it, a few words from Mother got him refocused.

Behind the township building was the former grade school building. It had been replaced by the new school just up the road. The new one was constructed in the early 1930s. I was in the former school a time or two, probably when Dad was a trustee. On the south wall of that old building was a blackboard on which someone had created, in chalk, the picture of a giant turkey. It was absolutely beautiful. The artist had used very expressive colored chalk. I have often wondered who the artist was. That beautiful piece of artwork was secluded in a building where few people ever saw it. I suppose there is a lot of beauty that is hidden. Sometimes because we are not looking.

On the westside of Palmer Square, just south of the church and township buildings, was a farm where, at first, the Doan family lived. Bob and Bill purchased an old Chrysler from Mr. Doan once upon a time. They left water in the radiator on a cold night. The water froze and damaged the block. The Doans were Christians but not Methodists. It was, however, at the Doan home that someone came to talk about singing and learning to read shape notes. I think the purpose of the gathering was to develop a singing school. But that would have required money, and there were just no extra finances in our house for that. There was no second gathering. The Doans had a daughter named Effie, who was about my age.

After the Doans moved away, Alvin and Leroy Ford occupied the place. They farmed. Leroy also owned a milk route. He picked up grade B milk. Alvin was my brother Bill's closest friend. Alvin was the brother of Ada, whom I mentioned previously, the one shot on Halloween. The Fords had a brother, Howard, who was killed in Australia during World War II. He was hit by shrapnel falling from the sky during some kind of military exercise. His death was the result of friendly fire. Later, Tommy Fisher and his wife, Gertrude, purchased the farm and were living there when we moved to Waterford. They had a daughter, Roma.

Just beyond Palmer Elementary School was the McElvane place. The McElvanes had a son about my age. I remember attending a birthday party for him. His mother served ice cream and cake. Mr. McElvane spent quite a while in a sanitorium. He suffered from tuberculosis and died of that malady. One Sunday afternoon, Dad, Mom, and I traveled to the sanitorium in the McConnelsville area to visit him. I remained out on a screened-in porch while Mom and Dad went inside.

This family attended the Methodist church some. One Sunday, Mrs. McElvane was accompanied by another woman who may have been her sister. That woman had a wonderful alto voice. Her beautiful voice enhanced all the singing that morning at the Palmer M. E. Church. I was impressed.

Farther south was the farm of Jim Murdoch. Jim never attended church as far as I can recall, but Jessie was quite regular. Jim also held a white-collar job in Marietta. I have already spoken about his wife, Jessie. It was at the Murdoch farm that Chester Love and I dragged the ensilage chopper into the state road one Halloween. How was that thoughtless act of minor vandalism just payback for how much I liked Jessie? Kids!

MEMBERS OF THE NEIGHBORHOOD

Farther south on the eastside of the Square was the Fletcher Reed farm. Fletcher and his wife, Lucy, were pillars in the church. It was a rare Sunday when they missed worship and Sunday school. Lucy played piano and sometimes taught the youth class. Fletcher sometimes taught the adult class, and he had a wonderful bass voice. I can still hear that booming bass as it rang out on some of the well-known hymns and gospel songs that blessed that place of worship so long ago.

The health of Fletcher began to fail not long after he turned eighty. He and Lucy rode with Mom, Dad, and me to a church conference one Sunday afternoon around 1940. When we came back through Bartlett, someone decided we would have ice-cream cones. Fletcher insisted that he would pay, but when he reached for his billfold, it was missing. He became quite agitated and kept referring to ice cream as "grease." Lucy said he might have left his billfold at home, but he declared strongly that he did not. It took a bit of time to get Fletcher calmed down. Dad paid for the ice cream, and when we arrived at the Reed house, Lucy asked that Dad wait a minute so she could check whether the lost billfold was in the house. She went in and returned quickly to say the billfold was on the mantel. In those days, his condition would have been labeled hardening of the arteries. After Fletcher's death, their daughter Margaret and her husband, Donald Love, moved in to help with the farm work. Their son was Chester, who became my closest friend. Don loved flying. A few years later they moved to Wichita where Don sold planes and gave lessons.

On the southside of Palmer Square lived the Knox family—Grandfather Harry and his wife, the parents of Harold. Harold and his family lived just up the road. This family also farmed. Harold and his wife raised chickens commercially for some years. Mrs. Knox was also a 4-H leader. One day she and some other adults took a group of us kids for an outing to Civitan Park near the fairgrounds in Marietta. It is amazing that after all these years I still remember that day. There was a mud puddle at the bottom of the kids' slide. The Knox family included three children.

All the family members were musical and often played for PTA gatherings. I have a feeling their pay was the honor received from our applause. My brother Bob worked for Harold Knox some in the 1940s. I remember one story he told of which he was an eyewitness. A cat had killed a chicken, maybe a young one. Mrs. Knox grabbed the cat and killed it by banging its head against concrete blocks. Bob was tender-hearted, and the experience upset him. Some years before we moved from Palmer Square, the Knox family named their part of the community Knoxdale. The *Marietta Times* carried a picture of the sign and a story about it.

It was at the Harold Knox house that I attended a 4-H organizational meeting. I had walked there as dusk was falling across the hills. It was summertime. By the time our meeting was completed, it was quite dark. A young male adult, whose name I cannot recall, took me in his car down to the road leading to my house and let me out. I had at least three-quarters of a mile to walk before reaching my house. There was some moonlight, and I was not overly anxious as I walked rapidly down the open road. But a quarter mile from our house there was a wooded area. Some limbs hung out over the road. As I reached that part, my anxiety forced me into a hard run. The various sounds coming from the woods gave me added energy and speed. I ran all the way home from there. I often wondered why the guy didn't take me home in his car. Probably because he could not spare the gasoline.

The Strauss family were the last locals on the immediate Square. They were a Catholic family, as I've mentioned, and they were great neighbors, excellent farmers, and hard workers. I remember Mr. Strauss, Carl, telling us one day during World War II that they had received a letter from one of their sons in the fighting. A bomb had dropped in, or very near, the son's foxhole. It did not detonate. As this grateful father, standing in our backyard, told the story, great tears of emotion flowed down his face. The offspring of Carl and his wife still farm the land there. Probably the fourth generation. Maybe more.

Other families in the area also blessed my life. Their farmhouses were not located on the Square, but their land either touched it or was very close. The Jess Stollar family lived near the Square. There were several children in the family. The two I remember best are Sarah Jane and Mary Ann. Sarah Jane sat just ahead of me in first grade. I remember that she seemed to delight in tossing her hair back onto my desk a lot. The family car was an air-cooled Franklin. (This car was manufactured from 1902 to 1934.) It was probably that vehicle in which an older daughter had an accident on a steep hill as she was going to or coming from Waterford. I don't recall that she was injured in a major way, nor can I say just how the Franklin looked after the accident.

I have a freeze-framed image of Jesse Stollar plowing a field with a span of mules. It was February or March in a year prior to 1942. I know that fact because the school bus was still coming down to our house to pick us up. That morning there was a light steady snow falling. The flakes were huge. As the bus moved along our township road toward the state highway, just north of the Bingham farm, we could see Jesse and the mules moving across the landscape. They were slowly turning the soil. When we came home that evening, Jesse was still at it. In those days it took a long time to plow a ten-acre field with mules or horses.

One of the most active families in the church was that of Lemuel and Lizzie Hale. Lizzie, her given name, was Sunday school secretary. Lem, as he was known, was one of the stewards. He passed the offering plate each Sunday. I have a very special memory of the Hales. At least one year they planted pumpkin seeds with their corn. They had hundreds of pumpkins left in the field when they had collected all they wanted. Dad and Mr. Hale must have talked about it at church, and one day Dad and I headed down the road toward their farm. I was probably five years old and not in school yet. Once in the field we saw pumpkins everywhere. So Dad put the little John Deere H in low gear, had me push the hand clutch forward from time to time, and we moved very slowly across the field. As we moved along, Dad grabbed pumpkins and placed them in the wagon. Now and then he would yell "Stop!" I would pull the clutch handle back and stop. We did this until the wagon was full. Then we headed home. I think we brought three loads to the barn. The pumpkins were fed to the cows. Lemuel and Lizzie's granddaughter, Sally, still lives on that farm. Some families just stay put.

The Cecil and Anna Sheets farm also touched the Square. I have already mentioned the New Year's Day dinner at their house. During the Second World War, I asked and was granted permission to gather milkweed pods from a particular place on their land. Milkweed was used, so we were told, in making life preservers for the US Navy. I was able to fill several bags with milkweed pods from the property. The bags were then hung outside on a fence as directed. There they dried for a period of time. We then took them to the schoolhouse, where they were picked up and delivered to the place where they were used in the war effort. (We were later told that the milkweed pods were never used.) Everyone was eager to be engaged in the effort to destroy Hitler and the Third Reich.

Palmer Square has changed a lot in the last seventy-five years. Many of the original houses have been replaced with new ones. Some are still crumbling in the path of time's advance. The elementary school children now go to Watertown. The building where I attended grade school is now a community building. The Amish are moving in. They have a store now on the Square. Too, I have a feeling that there are far fewer fences enclosing fields than in 1940. My Dad was once visiting my family and me at a place called Derby near Mt. Sterling, Ohio. A John Deere dealership was nearby. We walked over and saw a tractor with seven turning plows hanging on it. Dad said to me, "We didn't have a field large enough to turn that outfit around in." I have a feeling many of those fences are gone today. The Methodist Church looks much the same. But inside it is different. The members have worked diligently to keep it open and to upgrade it.

CHAPTER 9

THE CENTERS OF SHOPPING

THERE WERE BASICALLY two towns in which we shopped, if we consider Waterford and Beverly as one. This understanding those townspeople will probably never approve. Beverly is on the east side of the Muskingum River, and Waterford on the west. In sports the two towns are super rivals. When Waterford and Beverly played, those who wanted a seat needed to be there early. During the time we lived in Waterford, a young man by the name of Clyde Drake was the basketball team's star player. He was very athletic and must have set some school records. I attended a game that was unbelievable. The score was 102 to 17. I wonder how many points Clyde made that night.

Beverly is where Chandler's Kroger store was located. Mom usually shopped for groceries there. It seems strange now, but back then Mom took her list to the counter, and Mr. Chandler retrieved each item she wanted one by one. If she had cheese on the list, he would go back and cut some off a large wheel that lay on a cutting block in the back of the store. Usually a bit of visiting went on as he worked. One time I recall Mother saying something to him about the knife needing to be sharpened. His response was that one wanted a dull knife when cutting cheese. The store was not large. In fact, today we might shake our head and say, "Can't believe that this was a Kroger."

One afternoon or evening, Mother and I were in the store. While Chandler was retrieving something for Mom, an elderly woman entered and moved in close to the candy case. Mr. Chandler quickly came up the aisle and opened up with some very strong words of condemnation directed at the old woman. He told her in no uncertain terms to get out. Mother questioned his attitude. She thought Fuzzy (his nickname) had used language that was excessively harsh. He said, "She steals candy. She has that big loose coat on. She grabs the candy when I am pre-occupied, sticks it in her pockets, and then goes out and gives it to the children on the street." I would later learn that her name was Smiley. And I suppose she smiled a lot when she made a good haul while Chandler's back was turned. I have a feeling the kids loved her. I assume she suffered from kleptomania.

The Riecker Department store was another business we often visited. I remember Miss Nieb, my teacher at Palmer Elementary, telling us one morning that Rieckers had remodeled, and now the dry goods were laid out on stands just like stores in New York City. Actually, I believe Mom and I had been shopping at Rieckers the night that thunderstorm hit the tent meeting.

On down the street toward the Lock was Corner's Filling Station. Everet (Eppy) was the owner. I remember one day of being in the station. I must have been with my older brother. I began to play with a little machine on one of the counters. I think one put a penny in and pulled a handle. The pull caused three rows of icons to spin. If the rows came up with the same images all across, the payoff may have been a dime. The machine so fascinated me that I stayed with it for a long time. A bit later I realized the machine was probably illegal, a form of gambling.

Another time I was at that station when my older brothers were trading cars. I think they were trading their old Chrysler for a Model A Ford.

THE CENTERS OF SHOPPING

Mr. Corner must have been a notary public. He could, therefore, make the transfer legal. And on another occasion Dean Campbell and I were loafing around there one day when Dean decided to wash his bike. He had the water going full blast when Mr. Corner came out and ran us off.

Dean and I could provoke people sometimes. We left our bicycles on the front steps of Dillehay's Hardware Store in Waterford one day. I was looking for some Chinese Red paint. I purchased a small can. Then Mrs. Dillehay walked to the front of the store with us, and in no uncertain terms loudly instructed us to "Never park those bicycles on these steps again." We didn't.

Chester Mindling and his wife owned the funeral home in Beverly in our early Palmer days. They also operated a furniture store. Mom and Dad purchased a green living room suite from that store, two chairs and a couch. I didn't know it at the time, but later was informed that the furniture had been repossessed, and our parents purchased it at a very good price. That furniture was used for many years. Later, McCurdy purchased the funeral home.

The Muskingum Valley Hardware on Main Street is the place where Dick's sled and my wagon were purchased one Christmas. I was preschool age, and Dick was probably first grade. The sled I still have. The brake that Dick designed and attached when he was a child is still on it. Also, sometimes we stopped at Keyhoe's Meat Market and purchased something, although we most often used our own beef and pork. The stores were so different then. We interfaced with the owners. The Citizen's Bank was the same. Mr. Harry Yarnell was in charge of that facility for many years. I secured a ninety-day-note loan there when purchasing my first car. Later I received a loan from that bank to purchase a mobile home.

My brother Bill was a young man in a hurry. Recently he told me of an encounter with Mr. Yarnell. Bill had decided to quit school and purchase a milk route. He had the brass to go to the bank and ask to see Mr. Yarnell. He was taken back to the bank office and seated. When Mr.

Yarnell came in, he said, "Well, Bill, what can I do for you?" Brother said, "I want to borrow two thousand dollars to buy a milk route."

"How old are you, Bill?" he asked.

"Sixteen," my brother responded.

"I can't lend it," the banker said. "You are not old enough."

"My Dad said he would sign for me," my brother responded.

Then Mr. Yarnell said this: "If 'Aus' (Austin) Hill said he will sign, that's good enough for me. You can have the money."

I don't know how long Bill had the milk route, but he paid it off. He later purchased another. Sometime during his late teen years, he underwent a spiritual awakening, returned to high school a year or two later, and went on to graduate from Trevecca Nazarene College in Nashville, Tennessee. He has spent the rest of his life as a Nazarene minister. He died March 31, 2021, at the age of ninety-three years and ten months.

Webster's Garage was also down toward the river. On occasion Dad stopped there. I think that is the place where our six-volt radio battery was recharged when it died.

Also, down closer to the river was a blacksmith shop. When I was a child, that place really impressed me. The smithy wore a leather apron, usually had a fire going in the forge, and could make metal glow red in just a few minutes. Too, he could then pound it into any shape he wished. His work was fascinating. I think it was plow points that Dad had reshaped there when they were worn from turning soil.

Beverly was where the Henderson family lived. They had two daughters, Eileen and Imogene. My older brothers were kind of drawn to the girls. Bob married Eileen. She worked at the Citizens' Bank. Often, when our shopping was done, we would stop at the Henderson's just to visit. Their home was always warm and inviting. The family was a part of the Nazarene Church, and the pastor stopped by their house often. Most times he stopped by unannounced. The Nazarene Church opposed the use of tobacco in any form. Mr. Henderson (Rudy) smoked cigarettes.

THE CENTERS OF SHOPPING

On occasion the pastor's car would pull up out front. The pastor's arrival could be seen from the sitting room window. If Rudy was in that room, he would quickly make his exit through the kitchen and out the back door. I am sure he wasn't fooling the good pastor. He could read the behavior and, of course, smell the smoke. Rudy's mother-in-law lived with the family. Someone said Rudy on occasion would suggest that she was the smoker. I don't know whether that story is true or not. Rudy could be a bit devilish on occasion. He was a really good man.

On occasion we purchased some items from Vaughn's Store, which was located in Waterford, near the Muskingum. It was a large department store. During the months we lived in Waterford, I remember purchasing bread there for ten cents a loaf. One day as we drove past Vaughn's, there was a lot of activity at street level. Peaches! A truckload, and it seemed there was a rush to buy. But we almost always purchased canning peaches at some local orchard, usually up near Newport, and later at an orchard near Layman. There was another grocery store we sometimes patronized. It was next to Mason's Hardware. The places of business in those two towns serviced the needs of a lot of people and still do.

Sometimes we would stop and visit the Townsends, Harley and his wife, Ella Mae. They lived in Waterford. They had a daughter, Marilyn, who was very attractive. Bill dated her for some time. He took her to Parkersburg to the Nazarene Church during a revival meeting. While worshipping he noticed the young female pianist providing the instrumental music. He tells the story that he began to feel strange and couldn't figure what was wrong. After a few days, Ms. Townsend helped him out. "You have fallen for that girl playing the piano," she told him. She was right. The girl was Kathryn Johnson.

Bill and Kathryn were married Sunday, June 13, 1948, at the close of worship in the First Church of the Nazarene in Parkersburg. I attended the wedding ceremony. They celebrated their seventy-second wedding anniversary June 13, 2020. In later years, Bill was often in phone contact with the former Marilyn Townsend, who had spent her life married to a music teacher. Kathryn once asked him, "If you could have two wives, would she be the other?" I personally think the answer to that question is "yes." Kathryn was an excellent pianist and organist. She and Bill sang together, and she accompanied him as he sang solos. Their music is well known among many in the Nazarene Church. Kathryn died December 14, 2021, at the age of 90 years, ten months, and 27 days.

Near the Townsend house was a swinging bridge that was quite long and spanned Wolf Creek. It was high above the water. Looking back, it was very unsafe, and we should never have been on it. Some of the boards were missing. But, if one stepped carefully, a somewhat safe trip could be made. Many times, just for fun, we negotiated the open spaces on that contraption and made it over to the haunted house. I never saw any ghosts in the house. It was just an old homestead slowly wasting away, going back to the good earth like most everything ultimately does. Including all of us.

There was a high hill just above Waterford. It stands above the area where the swinging bridge spanned Wolf Creek. It was and is, known as Bebee's Hill. On an occasion or two, some of us kids walked up there. There is in my mind a freeze-framed autumn view of Waterford and Beverly from that hill. The leaves have turned to gold, orange, and red. Some have fallen. The church steeples shine above the houses and streets. It looks some New England village photos I have seen in magazines. What a restful place to visit from time to time, if only in my mind.

Several times each year we went to Marietta to shop, especially to purchase back-to-school items: overalls, shirts, socks, and shoes. Whenever we were in Marietta, Mother always went to the Kresge Five and Dime store. The candy and peanut counters were near the front door. Mom usually purchased some candy. Ten cents would pay for several pieces of that sweet stuff back then. I remember one day, when Mother was buying candy, for some reason I went on out the front door. Suddenly people where everywhere, and I realized that Mother was not with me. Suddenly

THE CENTERS OF SHOPPING

I was in a state of full panic. But just as suddenly as panic struck, I saw my mother's concerned and welcome face in the crowd. She was coming to rescue me. She didn't scold me. She did say to stay close to her. I was probably three. That memory is etched deeply in my memory. It truly felt good to be rescued.

Another freeze-framed moment in Marietta happened in 1938. Marietta was celebrating the 150th anniversary of its founding. Marietta was the first settlement in the Northwest Territory. I must have been thirsty because I entered the courthouse to get a drink at the water fountain. I knew where it was located. I was five years old. Before I could secure my drink, however, a huge "Indian," came to get a drink. He was painted red and wore no shirt. Also, he had on what appeared to be Native American attire. I gave him a wide berth. A real Native American? No, I have a feeling he was a white man playing a role that day. But at that moment he was real to me. I left without a drink.

There was something I did not know about that 1938 event. Of course, being only five years of age and my parents being Republicans, it may not have been high on their pyramid of needs. But a few weeks ago, Sally Hale of Palmer, sent to me a book titled *Washington County Remembered*. It was published by Ogden Newspapers in 1997. In that book, on page fifty-seven, is a picture of Franklin D. Roosevelt speaking to "an estimated 100,000 people" in the beautiful Muskingum Park, which is on the riverfront. All the celebrating was to mark the 150th anniversary of the first settlers arriving at the confluence of the Muskingum and Ohio Rivers. That bit of history is a wonderful story. Not for the indigenous peoples, of course, but certainly for the white settlers and their progeny.

Sometime about 1953, I worked for a water softening company in Marietta for a while. It was the Culligan Water Softening Company. I spent a lifetime on that job in just two weeks. Some of my deliveries were along Front Street, near the Muskingum Park, mentioned above, one place I remember very well. The cylinders of water softener were quite heavy, and the two-wheeled cart on which they were moved did not negotiate stairs very well. One house along that street was a real challenge. The last two steps of the basement stairs were rotted off, missing. I was in that house only once. How I made it down those rotten steps I do not know, but I did.

Another house, back high on a hill, was also difficult—not the house, but the woman who lived there. My boss told me that she always demanded a small cylinder of softener. But on this particular day he sent me up to the house with one of the large ones. There were no small ones available. The woman met me at the door. She was not kind. In fact, she was livid. She said, "He sent you up here with that one, didn't he?" I do not recall how I responded. She continued, "Just put that back on the truck. I don't want it. I will call your boss." I returned it. If my recall is right, I worked for that man just two weeks. It was a two-man job, and I was just one very young man. I think the moment my leaving was assured was the result of placing one of the softener cylinders in his little house. Somehow a few drops of water fell on the tile floor in the utility room. This woman became all excited. "I hope you don't spill water on other peoples' floors," she said. I think that was the evening I told the man I was leaving. It felt good to know I would not be going back on that back-killing job.

Mom, Dad, and I went to Marietta on June 6, 1944. We had first gone from our Palmer Township farm to Beverly. Dad stopped at the Citizens' Bank. He needed some cash. I am sure Mr. Yarnall was there that morning. As we were leaving town, just about where the Henderson house still stands, Mom began to talk about the Normandy Invasion. Her voice broke as she spoke about "All those poor boys who are getting killed today in France." She also probably thought if the war ended soon enough, Bob, who at the time was in training at Fort Walters, Texas, would be spared going overseas. That, however, was not to be. The war dragged on in Europe for nearly another year, and Bob would leave his life's blood on a French battlefield about five months before the conflict in Europe ended.

Our family once attended a circus show in Marietta. I was very young. I do remember the elephants parading around the center of a tent near where we sat on bleachers. The act that I most remember, however, was a young woman who entered the ring and began to slowly ascend toward the top of the tent in what I thought was a strange way to do it. She was hanging to a rope by HER TEETH. She actually did it. Or at least that is the way it looked to me. I sometimes wonder how Mother persuaded Dad to take us all to the big show. I am sure he saw it as a waste of money. Sometimes mothers have a way of persuading their husbands to do things they would prefer to skip. I have a feeling that was why Dad took us to the circus.

CHAPTER 10

LIFE CHANGED FOREVER

IT BEGAN FOR ME as quiet whispers between my sixth-grade teacher and someone in the entranceway. It was my brother Bill. Our brother Bob had been killed in France. The message arrived on Tuesday, December 5, 1944. Bob had been killed on Sunday, November 19. Life was drastically changed for me and the whole family the day that telegram arrived. It was an emotional tsunami that swept over us all, momentarily destroying all sense of normalcy and serenity, causing us to act as if our world had ended. All joy stopped suddenly. No laughter was heard in the house. Only mournful sobbing and utterances of pain. Actually, we were all in kind of a daze, shock.

When word of Bob's death filtered across the Palmer community, a number of neighbors came to weep with us. One couple came to assure Mom and Dad that they had not gone to the draft board to tell them he was no longer working for them. That had been a rumor. I don't recall Mom and Dad blaming anyone. Mom had some harsh words that she directed toward President Roosevelt. She blamed him for taking us into the war. I do remember that when Bill and I arrived at the house, Dad was talking on the phone to someone in Beverly, checking whether there could be a mistake in the telegram. Could they have meant "Jim Hill," who was from the area? The answer was, "No, Jim is fine."

When tragedy strikes, we often are seized by a powerful force known as denial. Sometimes folks never move beyond that paralyzing condition. I once read of a woman who after ten years had not changed one item in her deceased son's room. I knew a woman some years ago who never forgave herself for urging her husband to make a trip that could have waited. It was reported to me that he, a farmer, had been working very hard and was extra tired. But she urged him to go. It was a trip explicitly for her. He went and was killed in an accident on the way home. The accident was not his fault. His vehicle was broadsided by one who ran a stop sign. She never fully recovered. Sometimes it is easy to blame ourselves. It is more difficult to forgive ourselves.

One of the great agonies for my family and me when the sad news came was the fact that there was no body to see or touch. And thus, there was no way to fully put closure on the open wounds of our souls. Looking back I can't imagine why the pastor of our little country church did not at least hold a special service of prayers and readings at that time for the family and community. I am convinced that such a gathering would have been exceedingly helpful to all of us who were totally grief stricken.

We were invited to share Christmas dinner with the Henderson family in Beverly, Ohio. I can still feel the gloom that hung over that day. Mrs. Henderson had prepared a great meal. We were all there, including Eileen, Bob's wife of a few days, but it was far from a joyous occasion. It was a group of wounded souls huddled together around the Christmas meal, wondering what the death of this young man meant for us all. Just recently my living brother said, "Our family would have been so different had our brothers lived." Of course, that is a fact. In just nine months between December 5, 1944, and July 13, 1945, our family of four boys was reduced to two. And that kind of loss was common all over the land.

LIFE CHANGED FOREVER

By the time the United States government returned Bob's remains in 1947, many things had changed. Eileen, like most young people, came to realize that so long as there is life, one should try to live. By funeral time she had found solace and the hope of new beginnings in the person of a fine young minister. So I am sure it was stressful for her to attend Bob's funeral at the McCurdy Funeral Home in Beverly on a Sunday afternoon more than two years after the death. And Mother did not make it any easier for Eileen, for she was upset that this young woman would be getting married again. How wonderful it could have been if Mother would have embraced Eileen's decision and made her family a part of ours. Yet, I have never been a mother who lost a son and saw my daughter-in-law moving on with someone else. I did, however, have a first cousin who lost a son, very suddenly, and she and her husband were very supportive of their daughter-in-law as she moved into a new marriage rather quickly. But back to the story of other changes.

In the midst of our sorrow and turmoil, Dad decided to sell the one-hundred-acre farm. The place where I had been born. Where I had lived for more than eleven years. The farm that had provided so much freedom and excitement as I learned about my world and life. Now, seventy-five years later, I know why he made the decision and have known why since my seminary years. I also know why he should not have made it. After any life-changing trauma, one should not make a major decision for at least one year, maybe more. Many years after the war was over and other moves were made, Dad told me, "I had to get away from that place. Everywhere I looked I saw something Bob had done. I couldn't take it. I had to get away."

It is a natural desire to escape such debilitating pain. To run. To believe it will be better somewhere far away. Or maybe, just away. I remember a young woman coming to me one day to discuss a marriage that was not going well. It appeared to me that the marriage had been a mistake from the beginning. Not many days after our first session she called to tell me that she and her husband were moving to California. He was in service, a recruiter. The military was sending him west. "We are going to California to put our marriage back together," she informed me with much confidence.

I took a deep breath, paused a bit, and said, "There is only one flaw in your plan."

"What's that?" she asked.

My response was, "When you get to California, you will both be there."

In fact, a couple of years later on a December day, I was standing in the Hilliard United Methodist Church office. The phone rang, and Margaret Beal, our secretary, answered it. She listened for a minute and said, "He's standing right here." She handed me the phone. It was the woman who had gone to California to put her marriage back together. She and her husband had divorced, and she was ready to get married again. She asked, "Do you marry divorced people?" My answer was that I did, but we would need to talk before I could give her a final answer. "So, if you will make an appointment and come to my office, we'll talk about it."

"I have another question," she said. "Would you marry me on New Year's Eve?"

I told her that such a special time was reserved for my family, but if it were early enough in the afternoon, I would talk with her about it. "So, let's set a time for you to come in and talk about it."

"Well," she continued, "would you marry me in a covered bridge?"

Wow! I thought. *This is some woman.* I asked where this covered bridge was located. Now of course, I was biding my time, wondering what was next. She told me the bridge was located outside Canal Winchester. "Have you talked to the highway department about this?" I asked.

"Oh no," she said. "I am told there isn't much traffic on that road."

I immediately had visions of being in the middle of the bridge and a huge truck starting through. I finally told her I had declined to officiate a wedding on horseback, that I would not do so while jumping out of an airplane or racing along on water skis. Then I shared with her that I felt her request was in the same category. So no, I would not do it.

Without even a sigh she asked, "Do you know anyone who would?" I gave her the name of a friend serving in the area of the covered bridge. I hope she got married somewhere and is happy.

Well, by January or February 1945, a month or two after we received the telegram, the farm was on the market. It soon sold. Actually, Dad gave it away. Four thousand dollars for a one-hundred-acre farm with a good house and buildings. There was a new John Deere B tractor in the shed along with the H that we already owned. More than twenty milk cows as well as hogs and chickens. Everything needed to take advantage of the new economic growth that was about to take place. The REA, within a few months, would be bringing electricity to the community. But the farm was sold. By late April there was a sale. What remained was prepared for moving, and before the end of the month, we were living in Waterford, Ohio, just a few miles away. Yet, for me it might as well have been a thousand. New school, new kids, and new beginnings that were unsettling, to say the least. And one of the last major painful disappointments, I was told that my dog could not come with us. Town was no place for a dog. So, feeling alone and lost, I was in my new surroundings, floating on a sea of uncertainty without a compass.

By June, school was out and I had the summer to play. Dad had told me that probably some boy would test me to see whether I would stand up for myself. He encouraged me to protect myself. "Don't pick a fight," he said, "but don't allow yourself to be bullied." Things went quite well for several weeks, and then it happened. A group of us boys were playing basketball down at the house of my new friend, Wayne Styre. He was a year or two older than I, but he lived just across the Waterford High School grounds from our house. I no longer know how it started, but suddenly I was attacked and was flat on my back on the ground. The attacker, a bigger boy, was on top of me seriously beating on my body. He made one unfortunate mistake. Somehow, he got a couple of his fingers in my mouth. My instant response was to bite down just as hard as I could, and I did. He let out a great oath, went limp, and set me free. It was over. In the following weeks he and I became good friends. He was killed several years ago in an auto accident in Tennessee.

It must have been the next summer that a man who raised vegetables hired us to tie tomatoes. The pay was twenty-five cents per hour. The farmer made the mistake of telling us that there was just about enough twine for the job. It would be close. As the afternoon wore on, my friend became tired and came up with an interesting solution: bury the rest of the twine and go ask for our pay. I thought it was a bad idea, but he persisted, and I was easily influenced. So that is what we did. God forgive. I don't recall ever again being hired by that farmer.

After our move to Waterford, Dad was hired to work at The United Dairy Company. He worked in maintenance. He worked with Harley Townsend. I don't know whether he liked that work or not. So many things about those days are quite vague in my mind. I know my brother Richard (Dick) went to work for a man whose company gathered produce in the countryside and sold it in Pittsburgh, PA. Dick was hired to drive a small truck through the countryside and gather up and transport vegetables to the packing house in Waterford. There the vegetables were boxed and prepared for shipment. On the night of July 12, 1945, Dick was directed to haul a load of tomatoes to Pittsburgh on the big truck (ton and a half). I now know that he was fifteen years old. He had not been truthful when applying for a driver's license. I am certain that Dad had vouched for him. Dick didn't complete the trip.

I can still hear the doorbell ringing. It was a contraption that had to be turned by hand. As the outside handle was turned, there were clappers that banged against a metal bowl that was on the inside of the door. Made quite a racket. It awakened me, suddenly. It was about six in the morning,

LIFE CHANGED FOREVER

July 13, 1945. I heard muffled voices down below, but I stayed in bed for a while longer. After a period of time, I got up and went downstairs. Mom and Dad were weeping profusely. Dick had been killed up along the Ohio River near Newport sometime after midnight. He had gone to sleep, and the truck had hit a concrete bridge abutment. The load had sheered the cab off the chassis. He was killed instantly, and the boy with him (his last name was Cunningham) was critically injured. All this information was provided by the funeral director, who had made the trip to pick up the body. Fog had also been a problem. Even the funeral director found driving difficult, he said, because of it. Our world crumbled again.

We had moved to escape Dad's pain related to Bob's death, and now it was certainly pain time once again, and in a very amplified form. We had known Bob was in a very dangerous place. But we never dreamed that Dick, so young and full of life, would be gone as well. My dad questioned, for a while, his belief in God. He did not attend church for at least a couple of weeks. I am sure also that he felt a lot of guilt for having vouched for Dick on the application for his driver's license. And that was, probably, also the reason Dad did not sue the owner of the business. I was present as some men from the State of Ohio told Dad he could sue and take everything the man owned. Dad's response was, "If that would bring the boy back, I would sue tomorrow. But all a suit would do is cause more pain." Of course, that statement is true.

Dick could be funny and devilish. Dad had purchased new dentures about the time we moved to Waterford. One day Dick came through the kitchen and saw Dad's teeth soaking in a container. He took the upper plate out, rinsed it off, and shoved it into his mouth, then tried to scare Mother. I don't know what she said to him, but she laughed as she told the rest of us about his shenanigans.

Dick also liked nice clothes, and with one of his first paychecks he purchased a beautiful outfit: light tan corduroy jacket, dark trousers, and all the matching accessories. He went to a studio in Marietta and had a photograph made of himself in his new duds. He also had purchased a new pipe. I have that icon still. How different our family would be today if he and Bob had lived. Dick's girlfriend at the time was Peggy Ann Sleek. She was red headed and quite lovely. If I remember correctly, she laid one rose in his casket. The last time I saw Peggy was around 1950 on a Saturday night at the Torch Speedway.

I have mentioned the Waterford kitchen. Just off that room was a kind of pantry where we placed the refrigerator. Coe Allen, a man who worked for the gas company, came and converted that appliance from kerosene to natural gas. Soon after that was done, I realized that now we had electricity, and we could put a light bulb in this appliance so we could better see the shelves when we were placing food in or taking it out. There was a wall plug right next to the unit. So I took the cord, plugged it in, then went to find a light bulb. I was successful in the search. I returned to the unit, opened the door, and proceeded to search with my finger for the place where the bulb screwed in. The socket was hidden up behind the little freezing compartment. I soon found it. And when I did, the electrical charge kicked me back against the wall, and as I left the appliance I seriously scraped my hand on some metal outcropping of the freezing compartment. Like many times in life, I had not explored all the ramifications of my proposed action. I never thought about electrocuting myself. Had I thought for a moment, I would have left the refrigerator electrical cord unplugged until the bulb was in place. The reader, I am sure, came to that conclusion quickly. Well, I am a slow learner, but I never repeated that stupid action when replacing the bulb. Experience is a good teacher if one is capable of learning and if one survives the error. So be careful. Life can be dangerous.

The last time I saw Dick face to face was the morning before he made that fatal journey. Wayne Styer and I were coming up the street about seven thirty. We had trotlines in Wolf Creek. We had gone early to check them. We had caught a few fish, stashed them in our submerged fish box, and were hurrying home for breakfast. The two of us met Dick in front of the Waterford Methodist Church (now United Methodist). Dick asked us if we had been successful. We told him we had caught some, but that morning on one line was a rather large fish that had been mostly swallowed by a larger one. A really big one had been disturbed as we checked the line. We laughed a bit together, and Dick was off to work. I can still, in memory's eye, see him clearly. Young, handsome, talented, eager to engage life fully, smiling broadly as he walked toward the place where he worked. How much can change in a matter of hours. As Diana Washington once sang, "What a difference a day makes."

Earlier that summer I had attended the Bible school at Waterford Methodist. The pastor of the church at the time was a retired Baptist minister. He was filling in, for there was a shortage of pastors. Many were serving as chaplains to our troops fighting in the war. Soon a pastor by the name of Phipps would become the minister. I would go with Reverend Phipps to Lancaster Camp Ground for a week with other youth from the church in 1946. For now, though, it was the retired pastor. He was present to speak to us kids on eight of the ten mornings. I told a gathering not long ago, looking back to the summer of '45, I remember him looking like Alfred Hitchcock. He unpacked one scripture text during those Bible school days, dwelling on one small part each day, and repeating again and again,

> Come unto me, all ye that labor and are
> heavy laden, and I will give you rest. Take
> my yoke upon you, and learn of me; for
> I am meek and lowly in heart: and ye shall
> find rest unto your souls (Matthew 11:28-30 KJV).

Across the years that text slipped into many sermons, especially when I moved into an extemporaneous mode of delivery. I recognized the frequency with which those words appeared, but I did not realize the source from whence they came. Then one day as I was preparing for a special presentation, I suddenly experienced one of those "ah-ha" moments. It was the summer of 1945 when the words were first indelibly etched into my memory.

And no wonder. Those words met a major need in my young soul. I had lost my oldest brother in the war. The farm where I began life had been sold. I had moved from my school and community. My best friend, Chester Love, had been left behind, and I was even separated from my dog. In some ways I must have felt as if life were over. I heard not just the old preacher saying, "Come unto me all ye who labor and are heavy laden," I heard that call personally. For I had lost almost everything. At least I must have thought so. When I chose my craft for the Bible school, I chose to make bookends in the shape of dogs. Our Elizabeth has those bookends today. And I must share that I never grasped the psychological meaning of the bookends until this very moment. How strange I didn't see it before.

And now Dick, my brother who was three years older than I, was dead. His body lay in a casket at the McCurdy Funeral Home in Beverly, Ohio, surrounded by several bouquets of beautiful gladiolus, Mother's favorite flowers. Our family was present for the first visiting hours. So much about those days I do not remember. But there is one moment—one moment as authentic as a first-class video record—still running on the memory screen of my mind. On a regular basis in my home and church, I had heard a lot about prayer. We had actually practiced it on a regular basis. One text that was drilled into my mind was, "Whatsoever ye shall ask in my name, that will I do" (John 14:13). Could that be true? I wondered. Could that be true here? In this terrible situation? I quietly and hopefully walked up to Dick's casket. I approached it with great care so no one would notice, and lightly touched it near where Dick's head rested. With one hand on the edge of the casket, I sincerely and silently prayed, "God, touch Dick and raise him up. Give him back his life. You can do this. Touch him now! You can!" I don't remember how many times I prayed those words. I know I uttered those words silently again and again. And nothing happened. He was dead, and God couldn't change that. I was more than disappointed. I was shocked that God had not done as I pleaded. Dick was not only dead, but prayer did not stand this true test. The Bible did not mean what it said. Later, as I matured, my understanding of prayer evolved some. I still cannot say I fully understand it. I do pray, but I don't expect an immediate response on the part of the Holy One. I pray that God, That Something More who defies all definition and who is addressed by many names, will help me to understand my situation in life and empower me to make the best of it. Someone has said that "Prayer changes us, not God." That may be.

A few years ago I told my brother Bill that my faith, generally speaking, was formed in the summer of 1945. I told him that after struggling with all the death and pain of December 1944 through the summer and fall of 1945, I had concluded that this world is still a wonderful place, that life can be a joyous experience. But this world is also a dangerous place, and one can be wounded or killed at any moment. Even though God cannot prevent bad things happening to us, God is with us as we journey through all the grievous challenges of this life's experiences. There is That Something More (definition used by William James and Marcus Borg) present to hold us close in all the threatening vicissitudes of this life. Call that power God, Allah, Adonai, YAHWEH, or Other, there is "Something More" that is experienced only through the sensitive eye of the believing soul.

There was another truth I learned during the months I lived in Waterford. It had to have been the early fall of 1946, not long before my family and I left town. School was in progress once more, and being thirteen, I began to notice the girls. One gave me her bracelet to wear. That was just great. I strutted around as if I were somebody with that icon on my wrist. Then another gave me her bracelet. That was even better. Two is always better than one. But then, someone told the first girl that I was wearing another girl's bracelet, *with HERS.* The first young lady came and furiously ripped hers off my wrist. I just didn't understand. How dare she? But gradually I learned some of the finer rules of relating to girls. Can't say that I ever fully understood them. Then, in real life, God gave my wife and me four daughters. I can't say I fully understand them yet, but one does adjust after a while. And if anyone should ask about how I evaluate my life with five women, let me say this: I would do it all again. It has been a great experience. Especially our Friday night pizza parties when all the girls were still at home.

While living in Waterford I had an accident on my bicycle. It was after Dick had been killed. Dad and Mom were very concerned about me potentially getting hurt. So they held a fairly tight rope on me. But that evening, Dad was going down the street toward the farmhouse where we purchased milk, and I was riding not far from him. I still do not know what happened, but a man in a Plymouth coupe coming around a slight turn in the road hit me, or I ran into his car. I somewhat remember the big lighted instrument panel on the car's dash as Dad and the man rushed me over to Dr. Turner's office in Beverly and took me in a side door. The doctor must have looked me over fairly well and discovered only a rather deep cut on one of my knees. He addressed that wound with lots of iodine. At that moment I became totally awake. I suppose I had been in shock, but iodine applied to a cut knee certainly remedied that situation in a hurry. The first shock gave way to the second. One other small fact I remember about that night is that I was wearing white trousers. The right leg showed clearly that I had been wounded in some way. I'm not certain that Mother was ever able to totally remove the stain.

The next day, a man for whom I picked strawberries in season came and wanted me to work. I told him I had a very sore knee. "Let me see it," he said. "Oh, that won't keep you from picking berries. You can be careful." So I picked berries. He was a good man to work for. The story was, however, that he and his wife did not get along very well. They didn't speak to each other. And I cannot say that I remember seeing them engage in conversation. They spoke through their son. One very clear joy of picking strawberries there was that I sometimes started at 9:30 or 10:00 a.m., and lunch was provided. On lunch days there was always strawberry shortcake, and it was wonderful.

One day a friend told me about another grower who paid more for picking those juicy delights. I was getting only four cents a quart picking for the man who came after me. My friend told me the other farmer was paying five cents. So on a day when I was not working for my regular employer, I went to the competitor, five-cents-a-box man. And low, I was disappointed. The man handling the counting and paying process insisted that the baskets must be rounded up. When we brought in the boxes, he would empty the rounded up berries into a different box. I immediately saw that I was being abused. I was getting five cents for picking a quart and a half. So I never went back.

Later I would learn from a Meyers-Briggs Personality Test that my type is quite rigid. I believe a quart of strawberries is a level box. That to me is fact. When the old guy who was in charge told me it was a heaped-up-one-and-one-half boxes, I just couldn't accept it. For years I informed people, "When I get my ducks lined up in a row, I don't want anyone changing anything." Thus, if a quart of berries is a box filled to the top, then I cannot accept the idea that a box of berries has to be rounded up. A quart is a quart. No more. No less. Some wag created a list of prayers for all Myers-Briggs types. For my group, ISTJs, the supplication is as follows: "God, help me to begin relaxing about little details tomorrow at exactly 11:41:32 a.m."

During the seventeen months we lived in Waterford, I learned a host of things. One of the first lessons learned was that I had to make decisions sometimes that didn't necessarily please those around me. One day I was with my friend Dean who was an excellent swimmer. We walked down to the Muskingum River near where Fort Frye High School stands today. He took his clothes off, grabbed a wild grapevine or rope hanging down from a tree limb, swung out over the water, and let go. When he came up, he said, "Hey, come on in, the water is great." But I declined. The challenge continued for some time. I knew I could not swim, and I didn't know how deep the water was, but I felt it was over my head. I knew the odds were against me.

Many times in life I have faced challenges that I embraced with enthusiasm. But most of them were not matters of life and death. In fact, it has seemed to me across the years that about the time I get fairly comfortable with life, suddenly a new challenge confronts me. No time to relax. Even at 11:42:32 a.m. The problem is that some challenges cannot be ignored. They have to be addressed. On occasion we can do it with ease, like a little boy I once knew who, being chased by a dog, jumped into a garbage can and pulled the lid down. Sometimes there is no place to jump, and we just have to stand and face the challenge directly, with courage, determination, and hope.

I remember once in my first appointment as a pastor I said something a bit negative to one member about another. The other within a few days confronted me and asked if I had said that. It took a bit of thinking. I responded, "I said it. And I apologize." I tried not to make that mistake again. Someplace I read, "Don't do or say anything you would be ashamed of if it were reported on the front page of the local newspaper." I can't say I always adhered to that level of responsibility, but I always had it in mind.

One late afternoon, some of us boys were playing softball on the Waterford High School ball diamond. At some point during the game, three older boys came up the alley in an old Model T truck. It had a load of something on it. We could tell because the front end was elevated until it looked very strange. The cargo, however, was fully covered with a large tarpaulin. I, along with some other kids, was able to lift the tarp and take a peek. It was a load of watermelons. Beautiful melons. I thought the boys were going to share some of them with us. But they didn't. They just got back in the old truck and chugged away. They later landed in court. They had to pay the piper one way or another. They were hauled into court in Marietta. They had stolen the melons from a farm below Beverly. I believe it was the Story farm. One needs to think ahead about the consequences of one's behavior. What is done in darkness often comes to light when the sun rises, or when the canvas is lifted.

A man by the name of Johnson was my seventh-grade teacher at Waterford. He was probably seventy-five years of age. He was filling in because those who would have been teaching were serving their county in the military. Mr. Johnson had been around for a long time. He was from the "old school." The first day of school in the fall of 1946, he came into class, greeted us, read a Psalm (there was always a morning Bible reading, usually without comment), and said something like, "Now I am aware that none of you are ready for this. You are like a bunch of young calves being brought in off pasture and cooped up in a barn. It will take some real work by all of us to make this work." He then laid down the rules. Only one or two I remember: no gum, no talking. He probably told us he expected us to study hard, too.

As the weeks wore on, we talked and chewed gum. One day I thought my life was over. I had slid down behind a large book, maybe a geography book, and was blowing bubbles with my special gum. One bubble was nearly as big as a volleyball. Suddenly it burst all over my face. A girl seated about three rows away just lost it. She exploded with laughter. She could not control herself. All this while I was trying to peel the gum off my eyes and face. Suddenly Mr. Johnson said to her, "Amelia, what's wrong with you?" I knew I was dead. Gone!

She answered, "Wayne (the name I went by when I was young) just blew a bubble that burst all over his face." Oh, I knew now I was really dead. Why had I been such a dunce? Why had I not kept that gum in my mouth?

Mr. Johnson must have been kind of out of it, for he said, "Be quiet. If you had been paying attention to your own work, you wouldn't have seen him." And that was it. God is good!

Our class had not shaped up. We continued to talk and chew gum. So one morning Mr. Johnson came into class with a rather large paddle. It had lots of holes in it. Holes would make the instrument produce greater pain. He slammed the paddle down on his desk and said, "And I will use it." At recess I went down to the restroom, where I saw a high school student whom I knew. I was telling him about the morning. I told him, "Old Clease came in this morning with a new paddle. He slammed it down on the desk and said, 'And I will use it.'"

And at that very moment Mr. Johnson stepped out from behind a partition and said, "And I will." I could have dropped dead. The moral of the story: Be careful when telling stories, even if they are true. The wrong person may be listening.

Church became more important to me in those months. Mom and Dad attended the storefront Nazarene Church. I too attended there often. But I became involved with the Methodist Youth Fellowship and also attended Sunday School there sometimes. Another boy whose mother was associated with the Nazarene Church, also, from time to time, came to the Methodist services. I think he came with his older sister. His mother told the story that her son, a bit younger than I, had attended the Methodist Church on Easter. The next week as she was preparing to launder his clothes, she found a little cube of dried-out bread in his pocket. "What is this?" she asked him. "Oh," he replied, "last Sunday they had Communion at the church. I drank the beer and kept the bread." Children see things in various ways.

As I reviewed my attending the Methodist Church while Mom and Dad attended the Nazarene, I suddenly saw something that had not occurred to me. Why would they allow me to do this? I was twelve years old. They must have sensed that I was struggling to discover just who I was, or wanted to be, or where I fit in this new environment. And they let me make some decisions for myself. That was good parenting. Thank you, Mom and Dad.

My first movie experience occurred on a summer evening in the open air. It was a free event, as I recall it. I have no idea of the name or theme of the show. And I might have forgotten it altogether if our car had not been hijacked by the concrete approach to the ally as we were leaving. I can still hear the crunching sound. After the initial shock of it all, we climbed out, got behind the car, and pushed. Presto! The Ford was freed. I wonder if that precipice has ever been honed down.

I believe the movie we saw in the open air was probably sponsored by the Dixon family, who later built a theater on Main Street. The theater was a place that experienced a large number of patrons. My family and I had, on many Saturday nights, driven past that theater, as the many patrons were spilling out onto the sidewalk. I think on the weekends that place was filled with movie goers. There would be large crowds leaving about 9:00 p.m., but Mom and Dad forbade me from going there. Going to movies was a sin. We know, however, that anything we tell our children they cannot do creates within them an insatiable desire to see just how exciting that particular forbidden fruit is. So one night I was to meet someone at the theater. I made an unbelievably heroic effort to get there, but was a little late. When I did arrive, the girl I was supposed to sit beside had already taken up with Dean, my best friend. There they sat holding hands. That was not a good experience. All I really remember is that Gabby Hayes was one of the actors.

While I was living in Waterford, Dixons opened a restaurant that was attached to the south side of the theater. I was in that establishment the first evening it was open. And I still remember what I ordered. Of course, I probably had very little money, so decided to order a Coke from the fountain. The young waitress, I have no idea who she was, persuaded me to go "High risk" and get a Cherry Coke. She told me how tasty they were. I caved in to her entreaty. It was satisfying.

The Dixon family must have been quite progressive. They owned the first new style Studebaker car in the community. It presented us with an interesting sensation. We could hardly tell whether the vehicle was coming or going. It kind of looked the same before and behind. That company began operation in 1852 as a wagon manufacturer. It ceased to exist in 1967. I just reviewed a group of restored models from the 1940s and '50s. Studebaker did introduce a lot of new styling ideas for motorcars.

One evening while walking up a sidewalk in Waterford, I saw a bicycle sitting against a building. I thought it would be cool to put it someplace else and make the owner look for it. So I did, and then went on home. I don't know how Peter Moore discovered that I had messed with his wheels, but he did. He arrived at our house and inquired about where I had put the bike. Peter, Dad, and I walked back downtown. I remember mouthing off to my Dad in some rebellious manner. Dad gave me a little slap beside my head. I cooled down quickly, for that was only the second time he had done something like that in all my life. (The first time was when I was age two, and he tapped me on one of my bare legs with a weed when I was standing in the middle of a flower bed. He had told me to move, and I didn't. Then I did.)

As we approached the place where I had stashed the bicycle, suddenly there was a major problem, the bike was not where I had put it. Someone else had taken it. So I felt obligated to help find it. We finally discovered it, hidden behind Dixon's Theater. We were all relieved. And I couldn't believe what Peter did. He had some money. "Let's go over to Johnson's Restaurant," he said. I told him that I had no money. He responded, "I am buying." And he did. We both enjoyed sundaes. I have never forgotten Peter. He not only forgave me for messing with his bike, but when it was found, he treated me, the offender, to an ice-cream sundae. Theologically speaking, it was a very Christian act. An act of true grace. Peter and his mom and siblings attended the Nazarene Church in Waterford, which at that time was meeting in a room near the bridge spanning the Muskingum.

As I wrote those last few words, I remembered a young man by the name of Pete Ullman. I no longer remember whether he had been graduated from Waterford High School or was still an upperclassman. It was a summer evening in 1945 or '46. I must have heard an ambulance racing through town, mounted my bicycle and rode toward it. There was a little cluster of people gathered near Vaughn's store. There was murmuring about the possibility of someone in trouble up near the dam. It wasn't long before the ambulance came racing down past Vaughn's, made a left turn, and sped across the bridge. Again, I mounted my bicycle and rode over to Beverly.

Near the doctor's office a crowd had gathered outside the door. The door was open. As a large group of us stood outside the door, someone gave us the name of the one who was receiving artificial respiration. It was possibly a young man by the name of Pete Ullman. He had been swimming near the dam, and something went wrong. He was reported to be an excellent swimmer, but somehow, he had been unable to disengage from some very strong forces created by the rushing water. At one point someone stepped out the door and told us all to back up, to give the workers and the patient all the air possible. But in a little while we were told that Pete could not be saved. He was gone. It is always doubly sad when a young person leaves before their biblically allotted three score and ten, or a little more, has been reached.

There was an elderly, nearly blind woman who lived next door to us in Waterford. In spite of her very limited vision, she was a wonderful gardener. She kept the weeds at bay like no one I ever knew. Dad once said, "I think she may see better than she lets on." There were a few occasions when I became restless, and Mother would say, "Why don't you go next door and check on our neighbor?" (Mother called her by name, of course, but after seventy-five years I do not remember it.) A few times I did go over and visit with her.

One day she told me a story about a man who had been out West and had killed a rattlesnake. She added the information that he had sent her the rattle. "Would you like to see it?" she asked. Of course, what kid who has never seen any part of a rattler would pass up such an opportunity? So she went into the next room and came out with a little brown package. She handed it to me. When I opened it, the thing rattled like crazy. It really frightened me, shocked me, and I dropped it. I can still see her laughing. The contraption was wound tight with a rubber band, and when opened, it made a shocking, discombobulating noise that would unhinge most anyone. The force of surprise wields exceptional power.

I found that elderly woman easy to talk with. It may be that she helped me learn how to be comfortable with older people. That kind of knowledge served me well across the years in Christian ministry. I suppose that could have been a negative moment for me, but it wasn't. It was humorous and exciting. Truthfully, after the initial shock it was hilarious. It's good that we can respond to some of life's unexpected events with laughter. In fact, we live in an era when the world could use a lot of laughter, for anger and hate seem to be in charge at the moment.

Recently I was talking with a medical doctor who told me about a new patient who came to the practice. "She seemed to be one of the happiest older women I have ever known," the physician told me. "So I asked her about what made her so happy."

"Oh," the woman replied, "my husband died two years ago, and I have been so happy ever since. You see, he was mean to me. He beat me many times. So when he died, I was overjoyed." Life's negative experiences do affect us in major ways. How many years of stress and pain that woman tolerated! How many marriages are filled with pain and hurt because one of the team is extremely domineering and hateful? I wonder how many wives (or husbands) have said, "How wonderful that I am free again." Marriage often brings a surprise or two.

One day a couple who wanted to be married came to me for the first interview. The man had been divorced. "What went wrong?" I asked.

"Oh, when I got her home, she wasn't the woman I thought I had married," he responded.

I looked at his bride and said, "I expect there are a lot of women who could say the same about their new husband."

There are pleasant surprises and then, there are other kinds. And there are many over which we have little control. We, however, always have the freedom to decide how we are going to react. But that requires real determination and unflinching resolve.

A few years ago I was called to the bedside of a man who was dying. I had known him and his wife for many years. They found living together very difficult and living apart just about the same. So now he was dying. When I arrived at the nurses' station, I asked about which room he was in. A very compassionate nurse showed me to his bedside. His wife was not present. The nurse told me she had left the floor and was taking a walk. Within a few minutes of my arrival, the man died. I walked out to the nurses' station to share the news. Of course, I am sure the monitors had already announced his death.

One of the nurses said, "You stay out here for a few minutes, and I'll prepare him for his wife's visit when she returns." The nurse lowered the bed, washed his face, and placed two comfortable chairs bedside the bed.

When his wife came in, I told her he was gone. There was no reaction. We sat down beside his body for a few pensive minutes. She looked at him in silence. Then she looked over at me and said, "Well, I guess he'll never tell me to 'go to hell' again." Some relationships just never quite get all the burs knocked off. Unity never finds a place to live in some marriages and homes.

CHAPTER 11

A SECOND SEARCH

DAD HAD FLED THE FIRST FARM due to his unassuageable pain, triggered by Bob's November 19, 1944, battlefield death in France. Now our earthly possessions were being loaded on a truck. The "mover" was one of the Yost boys from near Barlow. He was a friend of my older brother. His old truck had no headlights. It was a "daylight only" vehicle. That seemed strange to me. Today he would not be allowed on the road with such a safety violation. We arrived at Waterford near the end of April 1945. Dick was killed less than three months later, in the early morning of July 13. Dad had fled his first pain in the preceding April, and now it was pain time again. I don't know how soon Dad wanted to move from Waterford, but probably soon after Dick's tragic death. Sometime in the summer of 1946, he found a farm that appealed to him. It was located halfway between Barlow and Watertown on what was then Ohio State Route 76. The farm was owned by an older couple by the name of Bell, who were ready to give up farming. Dad and the Bells worked out a deal in which our house in Waterford was traded for the farm. I am certain that Dad paid extra in cash. The agreement was sealed, and on a day about the third week of October, Bill set the milk cans off his truck and loaded our furniture on it (it took two or three trips). The transition from the village of Waterford to another farm was underway.

When we arrived at the new farm, the Bells's moving company, Marietta Westside Transfer, was still loading, so we waited until that work was completed. One fact I remember about the Westside Transfer truck was that it had solid rubber tires on the rims. I had never seen a vehicle shod with solid rubber tires. The truck must have been manufactured in the 1920s. But the surprising truth was it looked like new. It had been very well cared for.

When the former owners had finally vacated the house, we entered. My mother was in shock. The sitting room floor was a mess. It was higher on one end than the other. The library table sat at an angle, like the legs on one end were shorter than the other. Also, the floor was rough and unsightly. Dad and we boys went to work immediately. Dad hurried to Marietta and rented a large sander. We pulverized many pieces of sandpaper, coarse and smooth, on those unsightly boards. And when we gave up, the floor looked about the same. There was one difference—the nail heads shined more brightly. Yet, when the new linoleum went down, it looked better. We became accustomed to the leaning-tower-of-Pisa table.

Family is much more than how level the house floor is. Family is about love and caring as well as supporting one another. Remember what was stated on a previous page: "Those who have a Why to live for, can bear almost any How." So it doesn't matter greatly whether the house is perfect or not, as long as the family living therein knows its Why is to help each member seek for and move toward his and her God-given potential. Life is about people, not things.

One of the first tasks Dad faced was securing farm machinery. He may have purchased an item or two at the Bells's farm sale, but we needed a tractor. He first went to Marietta where he had, in the past, purchased two John Deere tractors. The dealer said Dad could put his name on the list, but it would be at least six months before delivery. The manufacturing community was busy changing over from producing tanks and war equipment to creating domestic products. Demand for farm machinery, however, was much greater than available supply. I think Dad added his name to the list.

He waited a day or two and made a visit to the Ford dealer in Beverly. The dealer there told him the same story: six months. As Dad walked toward the door, the dealer followed him and asked if he would be willing to pay extra if the tractor could be delivered immediately. Dad did not give the man an answer just then, but said he would let him know that evening. After supper that night, Dad sent Bill to tell the man it was a deal. I went along. Bill went to the man's house, knocked on the door, and told him it was a go. I do not recall whether Bill carried a check with him or not. Dad had been given a list of the elevated costs on tractors, turning plows, cultivators, and discs. All equipment was operated by the tractor's hydraulic system. That was on a Tuesday evening.

When I arrived home from school on Thursday afternoon, the tractor and equipment were sitting in the yard. Money talks. That whole deal had to be an ethical nightmare, I would think, for a Christian. Even an ethical atheist. And I am sure Dad lost a night or two of sleep over the decision, as well as having to cough up an extra thousand dollars. Yet, he had to have equipment to get things going, so he did what he felt he had to do. I guess one could define the deal as based on situational ethics. I expect that more than once Dad asked God to forgive him. Knowing Dad, I expect he kept asking. As most people know, it is much more difficult to forgive ourselves than to accept God's unconditional grace.

CHAPTER 12

A NEW SCHOOL

IT IS STILL UNCLEAR TO ME just how it was arranged for the school bus to stop and pick me up. A neighbor may have called Mr. Goudy. The Goudys owned the bus. That may sound strange today, but in those years many of the buses were individually owned and operated. (That practice would change in a year or two when buses became board owned.) Both Mr. and Mrs. Goudy drove the vehicle. If I stood at my bedroom window, I could see the bus coming down near the Brackenridge farm. I would then grab my coat and be outside when the bus stopped. On occasion, however, when I moved away from that window for a few seconds, I would hear the horn that sounded like no other, and I would dash out the door to get on board. One night I was coming home on the bus. We were just entering Barlow coming from Vincent. Suddenly Mrs. Goudy stopped the bus in the middle of the road. She opened the door, looked in the big rearview mirror at someone in the back seat, and said, "Get off." I had not smelled the problem, but she saw it. An older boy had lit a cigarette. Mrs. Goudy tolerated no negative behavior. And lighting up was in that category. She ran a tight ship. Good for her.

ROLLING HILLS

When I entered Vincent School, I discovered that it operated differently from Waterford. Seventh and eighth grades changed rooms to attend various classes just like the high school students. We even went to study hall. I don't remember how I found my way around that first day. I suppose some Good Samaritan took me under their wing and led me, or I followed the crowd. When we arrived at Mr. Harvey Graham's science class, I was surprised, shocked. He came in rather somber looking and said, "Books on the floor, get out pencil and paper, I'm giving you a quiz." My heart stopped. The book this class was using was not the same as the one Waterford used for science. As I was fretting and fuming about how unprepared I was for a test, a very friendly redheaded boy sitting next to me and sensing my dilemma leaned over and said he would give me the answers. I knew that would be cheating. But at that moment I was ready for any available help. It remains a mystery whether I actually received help from him, but it is a moot question. We both failed the exam.

Later in the week I discovered that he had been in the class for two or three years and was making very little progress. He was just waiting to reach the age where he could get a work permit and quit school. I guess the moral of that experience is "Be careful whose help you accept; make sure they are more informed than you. And in these days with all the conspiracy theories floating around, it is best to check all information at least twice, or more.

Vincent High School (grades seven through twelve functioned in that building) marks the years during which I moved from the seventh grade to the twelfth and graduation. Some of the events of those years were very positive and some less so. Looking back, I must admit that I did not apply myself as I could have or should have. Study was not paramount on my pyramid of needs. That may be why, when entering Rio Grande College some seven years after graduation from high school, I was required to take "bonehead" English.

A NEW SCHOOL

Actually, basketball was a major focus during high school. I was never a star player. I was sixth man on the team, expected to go in and play any position. Yet, when I started in a game, I was assigned forward position. The real joy of it all was being a part of the team. And I learned that it wasn't about who got all the glory, it was the team working together to get the job done. And that understanding has served me quite well across the years in church work as well as community and family endeavors.

As I write these lines in the late summer of 2020, it is quite clear that the USA must soon begin to work together if this republic is to continue. The next few months may very well determine whether this country holds together or fragments further. A democracy divided against itself does not have a bright future. Lincoln had it right when he said, "A house divided against itself cannot stand."

Basketball was so important to me that Dad allowed me to develop a place on the barn floor where I could play. Gradually I put some lights up so I could play at night. Many nights over a three-year period of time there would be several neighbor boys joining me on that barn floor playing ball. Looking back, I am more aware now as to why Dad approved of that activity. He knew where I was and was also aware that I could get into very little trouble playing basketball in the barn.

There were two boys who came to the neighborhood who became my friends in spite of the fact that they did not play basketball. They were being raised by their grandparents. Sometimes on Sunday nights, Mom and Dad went to visit with the grandparents, and we boys would see what devilment we could get into. On one of those nights, we were playing Wild West and using BB guns. The game had been in progress for several minutes. The two neighbor boys were on one end of the house and I on the other. We would jump out and shoot and jump back. Yes, shoot in the direction of each other. The game ended when I stepped out to fire. My mouth was open, and I was yelling when one of the little projectiles slammed into my open mouth, rattled around on my teeth, and exited.

It sounded like ball bearings rattling around in a metal cylinder. That was just too close. What if it had hit my eye? Kids are fearless and sometimes slightly insane, maybe more than slightly.

Scouting became a major focus for a while during my junior high years. I was eager to join. We were Troop 217, I think. I bugged Mother until she purchased for me the official uniform. Scouting was a productive adventure for me. We learned some military-style stuff, how to tie a lot of knots, and hopefully, how to behave. Some Scout teachings coalesced closely to teachings of the church.

Many of the troop spent a week each summer at Camp Kootaga down in West Virginia on Hughes River. The first trip there, I was supposed to pass the swimming test for my First Class Badge. The river was not very wide at the camp. Not really intimidating. We were instructed to swim across and back. I made it across quite easily, but on the return trip something went wrong, and I went down once, and then a second time. There was a raft in the middle of the river, and there were two or three Sea Scouts keeping watch. At least two of them jumped in and began the rescue process. I can still hear one of them saying, "He is still fighting, let's take him down 'til he relaxes." It was during that trip down that I saw all kinds of scenes from my life flashing past like a movie. But in a few moments I was on the riverbank spewing out water like Old Faithful. Someone said, "He really took on a lot of water." I did, for certain. A day or two later I came back and passed the test. Also, I found the Sea Scouts who saved my life and thanked them sincerely. Yet, it seemed such an inadequate moment. How does one say, "Thank you for saving my life?" Again I need to say a belated "thank you" to Jim Yost and Lester Seaman, for their truck transported us boys to scout camp each year. I think Jim Yost was usually the driver.

Vincent High School had a championship basketball team in the 1950-51 season. In the fall of 1950, Coach Graham lined the team up on the gym floor at the beginning of the season for a little pep talk. He said to us, "You are good enough to have a winning season with a reasonable level of work. But if you want to be a championship team, you will have to give it all you've got." We worked hard, won the county tournament by overcoming New Matamoras, and moved on to the sectional tournament. New Matamoras also went on to the sectional. They were very good. We had overcome them with some ease at the county level. I don't think we were overconfident when we met them again for the sectional championship, but they won by a good margin. And at the sectional level only the winner went on to the district competition. Following our loss, many of us gathered at the home of Todd Orndoff, in Vincent, and celebrated a very good season. Members of that team were Marvin Scott, Ralph Dean Barnett, Don Roberts, Marvin Metheny, Tom Barrett, Lawrence Smith, Carl Goudy, Johnny Gaughn, Donald Greenlees, Denny Graham, Charles Hill, and Darrell Knost. Todd Orndoff was manager, and Harvey Graham was coach.

There are two memorable moments relating to Vincent basketball that I want to share here. First was a car ride that I will never forget. Bob Williams, who left the team after a year or two, and I had just come out of practice at the high school and were starting to walk toward Barlow, which was a mile or two away. It was 7:30 or 8:00 p.m. (In those days high school teams were allowed to practice at night. I think that does not happen today.) A car pulled up beside us, and the driver asked where we were going. We told him we were on our way over to Barlow. He told us to get in, and he would take us. Once in the old car, maybe a 1937 Oldsmobile, we discovered that the driver was intoxicated, drunk. He put the pedal to the metal, and by the time we were coming down the hill after passing where the firehouse now stands, Bob and I were both aware that we were on a very dangerous trajectory.

About the time we entered the village, Bob said, "Get on the floor." We both got down as best we could. I knew there was a stop sign ahead where this road, Route 76 (at the time), intersected with Route A-50, now

550. As we approached the main road that runs from Marietta to Athens, Tink, the driver, held the gas pedal to the floor. As we crossed A-50 at Barlow, the car, with us in it, went airborne. Today I cannot say how we survived without being hurt or killed. Maybe it was luck, coincidence, or Providence.

Somehow, Tink kept the car from rolling, got the vehicle slowed down, went to the first road outside the village, turned around, and in a civil manner, delivered us back to the Seaman and Yost store. Harvey Graham, our coach, and some others were standing on the store porch. Mr. Graham later said that Bob and I were white as sheets. Several on the porch told us they could see all four wheels of the car as we passed over. If a truck or car had been making its way along A-50 at the time we were barreling through the intersection, I would not be writing these lines. How quickly all our lives could have been snuffed out. How many young people were not as lucky as Bob, Tink, and I were that night?

The second event I recall is a basketball game with Saint Mary's Catholic in Marietta. On that particular night there were three games: junior high, reserve, and varsity. For those of us on the varsity team, it seemed a long wait until our time to play. So someone suggested that we run downtown and get some beer. Off we went, running the better part of a mile, on concrete sidewalks. We secured the beer with the help of a "friend" who was of age. Then we went back to the bus and drank the beer, one bottle each. And when it was about time for us to play, we went in and dressed.

We were ready and able. At least we thought so. Yet, as play began, it was clear that something was terribly wrong. All the players were off focus just a little. Ralph Dean Barnet was our longshot ace, but he could not get the ball to connect with the net. Sometime during the first quarter, Coach Graham directed me to go in for Don Roberts, a guard. In the first play I stole the ball and raced down the floor at a fast pace, but as I picked it up to shoot, I lost it, and the ball went out of bounds. At half time Coach was puzzled. We were supposed to be much better than these guys, and they were making us look really bad. The second half was much different. At half time we were down by twenty points or more. But with a few seconds remaining in the game, we almost tied it. We failed, however, to redeem ourselves. We lost the game by a point or two.

Don Roberts was so upset following the loss that he rammed his fist through the visiting team's dressing room door. I mentioned that incident at our Alumni Banquet a few years ago. Even the mention of it caused Don some pain. It was hard for me to believe that after all the bygone years he was still sensitive about that night long ago when we blew it. Don died just a couple of years after that banquet. I regret even mentioning that moment of stress release.

Vincent had to pay St. Mary's for a new door.

On Monday evening, our first practice after losing that game on Friday night, Coach Graham had us line up as usual. He began by saying, "I know what was wrong Friday night. I know about the beer. My first thought was to call each of your parents and tell them what happened." My heart sank. My parents would have grounded me for as long as Methuselah lived. He lived, according to the Bible, 969 years. "But," the coach went on, "I decided not to call them. But if anything like that ever happens again, I will call your parents, and you will all be off the team." We never did anything like that again. We were ashamed that our thoughtlessness and immaturity caused us to fail and our school record to be tarnished.

A happier event connected to that basketball season was provided by the Seaman and Yost store owners in Barlow. The community was grateful for the work we did that season, so Jim Yost and Lester Seaman (others may have helped) arranged a wonderful steak dinner for the team. It was held at the Flamingo Restaurant in Marietta. Nothing was spared. It was a joyful evening. All of the team and the community were thankful for the store owners' gracious gift and honor to the team. That dinner was the finest I had known up to that time. Jim and Lester must have instructed the restaurant to pull out all the stops. I know you are both gone now, but thanks for that wonderful memory.

Mr. Graham was a carpenter and knew how to do fine work with wood. He created a manual arts class, and I signed up for it. During the time I was a member of that class, my projects were two end tables and a coffee table. I still have them. When the first one was completed, after a lot more sanding and finishing than I thought was necessary, it was ready to take home. Dad put it in the pickup and started home. He stopped, however, at Seaman and Yost's. He took the end table inside and showed it to all who were there. Dad was proud of what his boy had made. He also commented on Mr. Graham's gifts as an instructor. It really made me feel wonderful that my father was proud of something I had personally accomplished. His attitude made me want to do more, work harder.

There was another day when Dad and I stopped by that country store. Mom had given Dad a list of groceries that she needed. We were in our new 1949 Dodge pickup truck. As Dad parked the truck, he turned the engine off, looked over at me, and handed me the grocery list and enough money to cover the cost. "Here," he said, "you go in and get these things. If something were to happen to me, you would have to help Mom. Get used to it." Of course, I had bought some things before, but that day I saw my life possibly standing in a much different paradigm.

My dad and mom did care deeply about their sons. But both of us had experienced something that made us both a bit tense. One might say "jealous." It was at a time when Bill and I were both serving churches. Betty and I were visiting Bill and his family in Akron, Ohio, where he was pastor of a Nazarene Church. We were talking one evening. I suppose the conversation moved to reflections about Mom and Dad. I said to him, "I really get tired of going home and hearing all the time about how great you are."

A NEW SCHOOL

He responded, "Oh," with some laughter, "and I get tired of going home and hearing all the time about how *great* you are."

Our eyes were opened. We both laughed and came to an understanding that we were both loved, probably about the same. I have always been grateful that my brother and I had that conversation. It cleared the air. Even as I write these lines, there is a major smile on my face.

There is another frightening Vincent High School moment I want to share. It was several years after I entered that school. I almost always rode the bus, until I bought my Model A Ford, which I bought for fifty dollars from Mrs. Gahan and named The Hadacol Special. On this particular afternoon when I was still riding it, the bus stopped as usual at the top of the grade where our house stood. To get to the house it was necessary to walk across the road. As we are aware, all traffic is to stop and allow young people to get off the bus and move across roads or streets safely. I always took it for granted that if there were any cars behind us, they would stop. But this time as I moved out the door and crossed over in front of the bus, I stopped with a jerk at the left front fender of the vehicle. Why, I do not know. Maybe I heard some noise that alerted my senses. Maybe it was just some chance thing. Or one might suggest again that it was Providence. Whatever it was, it saved my life. For just as I stopped, a 1949 black Mercury four-door came from behind the bus and passed by at a very high rate of speed. That experience was truly frightening. The bus driver at the time, Lester Deming, and I exchanged startled looks. I probably threw my hands up in the air, then went on to the house. Had that car hit me, it would have ended my young life in a moment. That car and driver will get more attention as this story progresses.

Some of my fellow students will remember that I led a strike while in high school. There had been some kind of understanding that students with excellent grades in certain courses would not have to take final examinations. The rule was changed. Now everyone would have to take the tests. That was my understanding. I assume the rule was changed by faculty. I became upset by the new rule. I encouraged some others to join in a strike with me. So we made some signs and sat on the road bank just across from the school. Actually, just in front of the office of the principal, Mr. Loren Weinstock. A window in that office gave him easy visual access to where my fellow strikers and I were sitting. Sometime about mid-afternoon Mr. Weinstock came out to see what was going on. There were some hard words, and some of us were cuffed beside the head a bit. No one went to jail. No one was injured. We still had to take the tests. I remember Mr. Bill Cordray, the agriculture teacher, addressing me during class the next day in a harsh manner saying, "Hill, you don't have the brains of an old tomcat." I did not respond. Probably slumped down just a bit in my seat.

At the time I did not reflect on why I would do such a stupid thing. But in later years I discovered a reason. It's the Meyers-Briggs Personality Test thing mentioned above. When I am told something for fact, it is extremely difficult for me to accept a major change. I have learned along the journey of life that things do change, and it is important to roll with the disruptions, and to adjust. It isn't easy, only necessary, if one wants to relax now and then, or if one wants a friend or two at the end of the day. I learned a lot about compromise while working with church folks. The day it dawned on me that I did not have to control everything was a joyously freeing moment. Yet, on occasion, I have relapsed.

Some years ago, when I was a district superintendent, the parsonage electronic filters were not working. The serviceman told me the filters needed to be replaced with new ones. He also told me some parts needed to be cleaned up. He even told me how to do it. I followed his instructions carefully.

A few evenings later I came home. I assumed the serviceman had been there and had fixed the filter problem. But no, the electronic filters were not replaced. Everything had been changed, but not in the way he had promised. I blew a fuse. The secretary to whom I spoke thought I was truly a mad man. Yes, I repented for being such a rigid personality type. I wonder why God made me like this? As Frankie Lane used to sing, "This time He gave me a mountain." The older I get the lower the mountain becomes.

Many dangerous experiences occurred when I was a student at Vincent High School. One event was going with Bud Forman to Beverly one night. He had an old Chevy coupe. I don't know where he procured it. It had a transmission problem. Bud took the gearbox apart to repair the problem. When he reconstructed the mechanism, there was neither reverse nor second gear. Also, on this particular night, a tie rod end had fallen off, and he had repaired the problem with baling wire. Needless to say, there was a lot of play in the steering wheel. He drove us to Beverly and back. The wire held. I don't think I would do that again.

Another time I was taken totally by surprise. A couple of us boys had been somewhere with Tim Reese. As we were coming from Marietta down the hill that leads into Barlow, Tim was going at least the speed limit. Another automobile was coming toward us. It, too, was moving at a good rate of speed. Suddenly the car coming toward us flickered its headlights. Tim quickly did the same in the blink of an eye. Tim broke to the left, and Raymond (Pinky) Leasure did the same in the other car, and each vehicle passed on the wrong side. It was breathtaking. Tim said, "Oh, we do that all the time." I'm still shaking from that short moment of total panic. Both Tim and Ray are gone now. They were guys full of life.

High school is the place where many young people meet their life mates. That was true for me. As young as I was, there had been very few dates for me. I knew who Betty Maze was. I had seen her at church as well as at school. It must have been my sophomore year in high school that there was an all-county sing. That is, all the public high school choirs in Washington County gathered one spring afternoon at Marietta High School, rehearsed the prescribed songs on which we all had been working, then that evening gave a concert. There were about two hundred voices in that combined choir. It was a wonderful experience. I no longer remember how many numbers we sang. But I do remember some of the lyrics of one. They have stayed with me for a lifetime:

> It's spring again/It will always be spring again
> And robins will sing again/their sweet melody.
> Although December will surely bring snow,
> We must remember, it's just as sure to go...

After the concert, Betty Maze and I shared a seat on the school bus from Marietta to Vincent. We talked some, sang some songs with our friends, and enjoyed each other's company. Soon after that we began to date a little. But in the fall, when I turned sixteen and got my driver's license, we dated more frequently. By the time I was graduated in the spring of 1951, we were keeping steady company. Then in the fall of 1951 I moved to Nashville, Tennessee, to attend Ball's School of Technology. We both dated other people. We kept in touch, and I visited her the time or two I came home during those months. More will be said about our relationship later.

CHAPTER 13

A NEW CHURCH

CHURCH HAD FOR YEARS played a major role in our family life, and after attending a few Sundays back at the Waterford Nazarene Church, Dad began to shop around. He believed we should attend a church in our community. One Sunday he came home and told us he thought he had found the place we would go on Sundays. It was the Vincent Methodist Church. He found the congregation to be inviting and blessed with a warm and gracious spirit. And his selection was right. I enjoyed the sense of community and belonging that this small membership congregation provided for everyone who came.

Dad was soon named Sunday School Superintendent. He loved people and was easygoing, thus, people responded to his leadership. But being a church leader can present some interesting moments, and he experienced some of those from time to time. The organist was Ila Porter, a maiden lady, and a person who was committed to church music. I remember three or four of us high school boys going to her house one night, and she graciously helped us improve whatever song we were preparing to sing at a church gathering. She was always present on Sunday morning and played well, as well as the old pump organ could perform. Dad, however, wanted to purchase a piano and have it used for the Sunday school time. As I overheard it, Ila was not happy and she said she would not play the piano. And, of course, her salary was the honor of playing for church and Sunday school. I do not know the details, but the piano never materialized, and Ila continued to play the organ. Sometimes we run up a trial balloon and see what response we get. If the reaction is negative or a light shower falling on our parade, we simply pull the balloon down and take another path.

Dad was more successful on another small innovation he suggested. I don't know where he found the idea, maybe in some literature for rural churches. All activities of the congregation were held in the sanctuary. That one room was the only space available. (Some years later an addition would be constructed) So, the Sunday school classes were located in spots where they interfered least with each other. One class of smaller children met near the organ in two church pews. Both pews faced toward the back of the organ. Dad suggested one pew be turned so it faced the other so the children could have face-to-face contact. The teacher of the group, who had been a part of the church forever, said, "Mr. Hill, those pews have not been moved since they were placed there when this church was built." That sounded like a negative to him and to me. A light rain on the parade. Again, I do not know just what happened, but the next Sunday the one pew was turned. I never heard a word spoken about how it happened. Dad and the teacher must have concluded that changing a pew after a hundred years might not be an earth-shattering move. Those of you who know how some churches function will understand.

There were a number of members who filled a teaching role for the youth class, but Mrs. Smith was the regular teacher when I was there. She was low-key, knowledgeable, and kind. She showed love and concern for all of us. No one can ever know just how effective a caring teacher can be in helping struggling young people find their place in the world. Teachers for children and youth should be chosen very carefully. The problem is, of course, that in many congregations the selection is limited because those who should teach are not available or do not want the responsibility. Some most qualified may teach school. A few schoolteachers have told me that they have kids all week long and need a rest from such labor on the weekends.

Mom and Dad continued at the Vincent Church until Dad's death on February 6, 1975. He was struck by a car as he was crossing route 550 in Barlow. He was going from the Yost's store side of the highway to the post office on the other side. He was killed instantly. My family and I lived in Hilliard, Ohio, at the time. As I returned from hospital calls (I was pastor of the Hilliard United Methodist Church, a suburb of Columbus), my secretary, Margaret Beal, told me that I should call my brother in Circleville. He told me that Dad had been struck by a car and was dead. I remember walking up the hallway to share the sad news with Margaret. She took one look at me and said, "Go back to your office and let yourself cry." I don't know that I did. Later that day I met my brother and his wife in Circleville, and we drove together to support Mom and share the pain. Betty stayed in Hilliard to look after our children.

Dad had fathered a child before he and Mom were married. The mother of the baby was Grandmother Hill's hired girl. The girl was a bit younger than Dad. Before the birth of the child, Grandmother arranged for Dad to go west and work for his uncle in the oil fields of Kansas and Oklahoma. As soon as Dad was gone, Grandmother Hill went to the girl, paid her an amount of money, brought the baby home with her, and raised him as her own child. In fact, I learned early on to call him Uncle. And that understanding did not change until after Grandmother died. Some legal papers came to the house for Dad to sign. I was looking through them, and although there were three of Dad's brothers' names—Aaron, Lloyd, and William—on the documents, Russell did not appear. I was confused. So I asked Mother about the discrepancy. "Don't you know about Russell?" she responded.

"How would I know about Russell? No one ever told me anything unusual about him," I said. She then told me the story. I was furious. Why was I kept in the dark for nineteen years? Why didn't I do the math? However, I gradually adjusted. Of course, in the midst of my shock I did do the arithmetic. And nothing added up. I am sure that it was no secret in Ritchie County, West Virginia.

Grandmother named this child Russell. He was a good person. Gifted. Spent time in the United States Military as did our dad. Russell was very interested in radios. He built one as they say, "from scratch," when he was just a child. After his time with the military, he went on to enjoy a lifetime in the radio and television business. He even invited me to come and work with him. Had I known who he was at the time, I might very well have gone, for I had taken a home course in radio. But I didn't know he was my half-brother. Truth is, Mother was always uneasy around Russell. Dad, knowing that, never worked toward making him a part of the family. My brother Bill told me that to be a part of our family was all Russell wanted. I remember a visit from Russell, his lovely wife, and his two sons when we lived on the second farm. Dad took one of those boys, maybe the youngest, six or seven years of age, and was holding him on his lap. Mom said, "Austin, you ought not to be holding that big boy on your lap. You might hurt yourself." That boy was not big. Mom never forgave Dad for his breach of trust before they married. Yet, she knew the truth before she said "I do."

Sometimes it is well just to let some things slide, but most times it is important to clear the air with confession, discussion, and resolution before moving on to some great commitment. Ironically, Dad was killed while crossing the road to the Barlow Post Office. He wanted to see if he had received a letter from the woman who had borne the child. He once told me, "If I don't get her forgiveness for this terrible sin I committed, it will be the first issue confronting me when I meet the Lord." Truth, the whole truth, and nothing but the truth, as well as forgiveness early on in

A NEW CHURCH

the drama would have meant freedom for all parties involved. I know the above letter information to be true, because I found some of the correspondence as I was preparing the property for a new owner. I also communicated with Russell's mother after finding the correspondence. She had forgiven Dad years ago, she said, had married, and enjoyed a wonderful life. She too is now gone.

I shall never forget that Barbara, our second daughter, a student at Hilliard High School, was on a trip to Washington, DC, at the time of Dad's sudden death. She had left on Sunday and was returning on Friday. Dad was killed on Thursday. So we went to Port Columbus (now John Glenn International), picked Barbara up, and headed for Barlow. Looking back, there wasn't time to let Barbara share any joy of her trip, for I was in tears when she came off the plane. In retrospect, it is possible that I could have handled that moment more compassionately. But even after all these years, I really don't know how.

The family gathered on Friday evening at the McCurdy Funeral Home in Beverly. Some of the good folks from my Hilliard United Methodist Church came for visiting hours, and others attended the funeral. One of my first cousins from Parkersburg, West Virginia, was there. She asked me a few years ago if I recalled what she told me that night. I did not. "I told you," she said, "I wish it were me lying in that casket instead of Uncle Austin." She then went on to tell me how troubled her marriage had been, that many a night her husband would get drunk, come into the bedroom with a gun in his hand, and threaten to kill her. She would call the police. They would come and arrest him, and she would go the next day and get him out of jail. I asked why she didn't divorce him. She replied, "I made a vow before God. And I could not break it."

Of course, I too am a Christian, but the God whom I know through Jesus the Christ would not demand such commitment from her or anyone else. My mother and I used to discuss this subject. She was opposed to all divorce. I would tell her that a person was quite capable of making a mistake in marriage just like one can in any other life decision. Yes, marriage is sacred, but so is one's life. And if marriage is destroying one's life, it is better to divorce and try again or remain single.

Edgar Lee Masters in his anthology about Spoon River, a fictional town, speaks to this issue as he introduces the reader to Rev. Lemuel Wiley and the Blisses. In one short poem the good pastor is elated that he was successful in persuading the Blisses not to divorce. In fact, he states that it was his greatest achievement. Yet, Mrs. Bliss has a different take on his work. She tells us that one child sided with their dad and one with her, and that family life was a mess. Mrs. Bliss near the end of the poem states:

> Now every gardener knows that plants grown in cellars
> or under stones, are twisted and yellow and weak.
> And no mother would let her baby suck
> Diseased milk from her breast.
> Yet preachers and judges advise the raising of souls
> Where there is no sunlight, and only twilight,
> No warmth, but only dampness and cold---
> Preachers and judges!

Divorce is seldom, if ever, a pleasant choice. But sometimes it is the best choice, for staying together for the children's sake can be very destructive to the whole family.

Dad's sudden death was a terrible blow for our family to absorb. His service was held at the Vincent United Methodist Church, a place he and Mom loved. My district superintendent, The Reverend Glenn Copeland, drove from Lancaster to Vincent for the service. He came in and sat near the back of the sanctuary. When I saw him, I invited him to come and sit with family. He resisted some, but it was a comfort to have him present. The pastor of the church read a lot of scripture, but that was about all. He said nothing, as I recall, about how much Dad had contributed to that congregation. He had been Sunday School Superintendent, teacher, trustee. He had supported every minister that came. Some were easier to support than others. Yet, everyone knew Dad was a good man, not perfect, and were grateful to have known him.

After Dad's death, Bill and I talked about how to help Mother. We decided to keep everything as normal as possible, at least for a while, and she agreed. That first summer we planted the garden as Dad always had. I can still remember the first day I got his old push plow out to make some furrows for planting. As I took hold of the handles, goosebumps suddenly stood up on my arms. Something unusual was happening. It was as if Dad's very life spirit was touching me. For a moment I hardly knew what to make of the experience. I finally just smiled to myself and assumed it was one of those moments that cannot be easily explained.

Our plans worked well for quite a while, but when there was a rainy Monday, our every-other-Monday schedule became a challenge. And sometimes I was responsible for a Monday funeral. If we didn't get there on the scheduled day, Mother might call and tell us that the weeds in her garden were really bad. "What will the neighbors think?" she would ask. So, after two years we moved her to Circleville to be close to Bill. That was where she spent the last years of her life. Several of those years in a rest home.

We placed her in Brown Memorial Home only after she experienced some kind of stroke and lay on the floor for many hours before Bill found her. When she was about to be released from the hospital, the doctor said to Bill and me, "You boys know your mother cannot be left alone, don't you? She will have to have constant care." Oh, that was a shock. We should have known. We would have known had she not been *our* mother. We just knew that she was invincible. Because both of us were always on the go in our pastoral work, it was best for her to be in a place where she would be cared for around the clock. Neither of our wives were up to looking after her. So we took her to Brown Memorial Home in Circleville. Mother had said to me once, "Will you promise me that you will never put me in a rest home?" And my response to her entreaty was truly difficult to give. But I said, "Mom, I cannot make that promise. I will do my best, but I cannot promise that I will never put you in a rest home." She didn't mention it again. The end-of-life-years are often very sad.

Almost every community has certain skeletons that get buried and mostly forgotten. Dad and Mom had noticed that two sisters attended Vincent Methodist Church most every Sunday, sat in the same pew, opposite ends, and seemed never to speak to each other. There came a Sunday when one of the sisters needed a ride home. We would be driving right past her house, so Dad invited her to ride with us. As we moved along in the car, Dad asked something about her and the sister. We got an earful. She said, "My sister and her husband (a well-known man and woman in the community) stole my inheritance. They stole the farm, which should have gone to both of us. I was left with nothing." We could not fully comprehend how difficult it would be to forgive such blatant behavior on the part of a sister and her husband. Only those who have experienced such loss could understand. Yet, even in a situation so grievous, forgiveness is the only road to personal freedom. The sister and husband had not only taken the farm, she, by never forgiving, had allowed them to also take away her peace of mind. To hold a grudge is to be held prisoner by our own refusal to forgive, erase the slate, and be free to move on.

Vincent United Methodist Church closed a few years ago. It was a sad day for many. A new group, maybe more progressive, had become members, and wanted to relocate. And there were good reasons for making a move. The proposal to close the old building and build a new one with more space for parking was approved. The motion was, however, approved by a margin of one or two votes. A close vote on such an issue is never good. When I heard the church was closing, I called Janice McVicar McGregor, a longtime member, and asked if she could arrange for me to preach one Sunday before the end. Although as a teenager I had spent several years in that congregation, I had never been invited to speak there. She gave me a date to come. I then called the pastor, who, I am sure, was under a lot of pressure. She really didn't want me to come. I think she thought my goal was to present a way to reverse the congregation's decision to move. My purpose was to share with those present just how much that congregation had meant to me when I attended there as a teenager. Also, to share with them how that church still lived in my memory and my approach to life. Finally, she invited me, but said she would not be there. I pleaded for her to be present. She came and participated in the service. But it was a sad day. Not because of the move, but because that decision divided the congregation.

That day Janice gave me a large picture of the little church. She, a local historian, had given it to the congregation and said she wanted me to have it. I am grateful for the gift, Janice. Last I knew, the new congregation was less successful than they had hoped and had returned to the building they had abandoned. Some dreams never come to fruition. Others just take longer than expected. I hope Vincent United Methodist Church's dream of greater expansion and success soon comes to full fruition and thrives. Janice and her husband, Miles, have both gone on to their reward.

CHAPTER 14

THE SECOND FARM AND MY TEENAGE YEARS

NOT LONG AFTER ARRIVING at the new farm, Dad and Mom were faced with the task of securing livestock and all the equipment needed to make the place go. There was a lot of activity as Dad secured milk cows, chickens, and pigs. All that transitional activity is still a blur in my mind. Gradually it all began to fall into place. The corn was planted, and I was cultivating it with the Ford tractor. There was hay to be harvested. That first summer the hayfield was close to the house, so we used a buck rake to bring the hay to the barn. That process was neat. Rake the hay into windrows, then gather it onto the buck rake, lift the front of the contraption hydraulically, and head for the barn. Because of the rake's width, I had to be very careful when moving through the gates. A time or two one of the rake's teeth did get hooked on a fencepost, but because of my constant vigilance nothing was damaged. I thought it was fun. Dad was trying to put the hay away in the mow, and I was just about inundating him. He told Mom he was exhausted just trying to keep ahead of me. I was nearly fourteen and full of energy.

Early in our time at this farm, Dad had a pond built. The Barlow-Vincent Fire Department had just been formed. Their first pumper was on a trailer that was pulled by a car or pickup truck. I saw the pumper perform at the farm one evening. It could spray water a long distance. Actually, it took a strong person to hold the nozzle end of the hose when the pressure was fully on. Because of the emphasis on fire protection, many farmers chose to build ponds as water sources for emergencies. Our pond was shared for fire protection with the Worthington family. I think Husky shared in the cost. Some of us farm boys tried to swim in a couple of these ponds, but the mud was too much. A long way from being lovely beaches.

At the beginning of my high school years, I became a member of the Future Farmers of America (FFA). It was assumed by many that one who was raised on a farm would grow up to be a farmer. I was, at that time, one who believed that. I had two animals for my FFA projects. First was a Hereford hog. This animal was red with a white belt around her body. The Hereford was derived from Duroc, Poland China, and maybe Chester White lines, so I have read. The Hereford line was different. Maybe that is why I chose it. There was, however, a major problem with this animal. When she had been bred, I waited for a litter of piglets, and she delivered one. That is, one piglet. The second round she delivered two. So, off to the stock sale she went.

My second project was a Shorthorn heifer. I was once again looking for something different from the Herefords, Angus, etc. But the Shorthorns did not gain weight and grow as fast as some others. So I discontinued that project. Unrelated to school, I made a decision somewhere along the way to raise rabbits. Dad and I built a proper hutch with individual units in which to keep them. There was a problem with the rabbits. I did not want to kill them for Sunday dinner, and I did not want to sell them to someone else for their Sunday dinner. That project, too, was dropped. Yes, by then I should have thought about something besides farming for my life's work.

My Grandmother Hill gave me two lambs to aid in starting a herd of sheep. That went pretty well. They grew, more lambs were born, wool

THE SECOND FARM AND MY TEENAGE YEARS

was produced and sold. These sheep were Horned Dorset. Grandmother raised them because she believed they were more able to resist dogs. Her sheep ran loose back on a mountain, and dogs were sometimes a problem. Sheep seldom move alone. They move as a group. And they are not really a formidable foe for a pack of dogs. Often, they put up no fight.

One summer evening my sheep came into the barnyard from being back in the pasture field. I hadn't looked closely at them for several days, so I went down to look them over. I immediately saw that one of the younger ones had an extremely swollen face. Not only was its face bulging out, but its right eye was swollen totally shut. Silas ("Si") Woodruff, a neighbor, had gone to Ohio State University School of Veterinarian Medicine and taken a kind of short course in that discipline. He helped a lot of farmers in the area with their animals. I went down to see Si. "Oh," he said, "that sheep has been nibbling grass back along one of those rock ledges and has nudged a copperhead, and the snake popped him." He gave me a bottle of some kind of solution and told me to work some of it into the wool on the side of the sheep's swollen face until the solution reached the skin. He instructed me on how often to repeat the process. I did as he instructed. For the next few days some very repulsive discolored fluid seeped up out of the wool. The swelling, however, in a few days, began to disappear, and the sheep seemed good as new. I hope he was more careful with his nibbling habits after that.

There was no silo on this farm, so about all the corn we raised was used to feed the animals in ground form. Not long after taking possession of the farm, Dad purchased a new hammer mill. We could grind a lot of grain in a short time with that machine. Our Ford tractor was the power source. One day while we were grinding, I stuck my head in a wheat bin enclosure near the hammer mill to look for something, and was shocked to see a sizable black snake climbing one of the walls. I turned away for a moment, I suppose, to find something with which to conk him, and then returned. The snake was gone. He knew he was in danger I suppose.

I suspect he stayed around that place, out of sight, for a period of time. I never encountered him again. I hope he captured a few rodents.

Snakes can be found in most any area of a farm. Actually, there are some very small specimens around the house in which we now live. And we are in the city. I saw one last summer resting on a shrub limb. I was trimming a bush nearby, and he just lay there and watched me. Of course, the ones we see now are very small and often super fast.

One morning following a hard rain, Bill and I walked to the back of our farm to check on the water gaps. There was one gap which often, after a hard rain, opened a pathway for the cattle to get out and go visiting in some neighboring field. On this morning the creek had not totally settled down, so Bill and I were picking up rocks and placing them in the creek as stepping-stones so we could access the water gap without getting our feet wet. This process was going fine until I saw Bill bend over to pick up a rock and suddenly freeze in place, then slowly reverse his motion and step gently back toward me. "There is a huge snake lying over there," he said as he came close and pointed to the spot. We had brought a bucket with us which contained staples, nails, hammer, and a hatchet. Bill took the hatchet, cut a moderate-sized limb off a sycamore tree that was overhanging the creek, and headed back toward the snake. He hit the viper with a very determined blow. The snake stood up about two feet several times. He was not going to go to snake heaven without a reasonable fight. Bill hit it a few more times and killed it. We did not determine what kind of viper it was. The head was large and V-shaped, indicating it was poisonous. Maybe some kind of water moccasin. It was huge. After the crisis had been taken care of, we made it to the fence gap and repaired it. We then picked up our tools and moved back toward the house, glad to be out from under the rock cliff, which we knew housed some of the largest copperheads in the area.

One Mr. Porter, who dug mayapple and ginseng on our farm, told Dad once that he had observed the largest copperhead he had ever seen, near that rock ledge just above the creek. I know that in some later years Dad was along that ledge gathering rocks to reinforce one of the entrance ways into the barn. He told me that he had lifted a number of rocks up with his shovel and found more than one copperhead there. He killed them. Sorry.

One summer day I was baling hay. The sun was shining, and the weather was really hot. It was midafternoon. When running the baler, it was important to watch the feed pickup to make sure the hay was properly entering the baler. As I was going down a long sloping part of a certain field, some movement near the rear of the baler caught my eye. I took a closer look. I couldn't believe what I was seeing. I blinked my eyes a bit and took a second look. A large black snake was moving down the field with me while staying in the shadow of the baler. It was a sight hard to process. I watched him for several minutes with focused interest. If I slowed down, he slowed too. The noise seemed not to faze him. He stayed right in the baler's shade, whatever speed I was going. And when I came to a low place in the field and started up the long, low incline ahead, he veered off into a nearby area of grass and shrubs and was gone. I never saw anything like that again. He was a shade seeker and didn't seem to care where he found it. There may be a life lesson in that story, but I haven't yet discovered it.

Then there was the day Dad and I were picking blackberries. The land belonged to Si Woodruff. Somehow Dad had discovered this bottomland that had laid fallow for years. A few cattle grazed there in summer. There were acres of wild blackberry vines in the field. So Dad arranged for us to pick some of the berries. I still remember on the very first day I was picking away at a vine simply loaded with large juicy fruit. I was picking with a small bucket secured with a piece of soft rope around my neck. That allowed both my hands to be free for work. As I picked away with my eyes focused on the next vine, Dad came quietly up beside me and said, "Why don't you turn around and pick on that bush over there." He pointed to a vine just behind me. It, too, was loaded with very large berries. There was a cow path that separated the two clumps of vines. I thought nothing about it, just turned and resumed my work.

We picked in that field for at least three days. Mom prepared and froze the berries. She may have made some jam out of a few. On the evening after we had completed the berry picking and were relaxing and eating supper, Dad said to me, "Do you remember the first day we were in the berry patch, and I suggested that you turn and start picking on the other side?" I told him I remembered. "Well," he said, "just in front of you in that patch of berries laid one of the biggest black snakes I have ever seen. And I knew if you saw it, all berry picking for you would be over." We both had a good laugh. I'm glad I didn't know. Sometimes what we don't know won't hurt us. Of course, the opposite is also true.

There were other animals that could make farm life a challenge. Groundhogs are one group in that category. These rodents are sometimes entertaining to watch, but they can dig holes deep enough to cause havoc when one is cutting hay or working in some other way, such as plowing ground. More than once in a particular field I experienced a sudden drop of a tractor wheel. When such a surprise drop occurs, it can throw the driver out of the tractor seat. Dangerous.

One day Dad and I were walking toward the back side of the farm. At a particular place where a large curly maple stood near a gate, we encountered one of these rodents. Up the tree he went. Yes, I know they are not known for climbing, so far as I know, but the trunk of the tree was large, and the first limbs quite low. The hog made it up to the first limb and just sat there looking down at us. We had two dogs with us. They went bananas. Suddenly the groundhog jumped down and tried to run away. The dogs caught up with him. One grabbed the head, the other his tail. They shook this animal until they were exhausted. When they put him down, he began to slowly walk away. I don't know how many times this process was repeated. The animal, however, finally gave up the ghost.

THE SECOND FARM AND MY TEENAGE YEARS

Looking back, we should not have allowed this carnage to go on as it did. But groundhogs and farmers are generally not friends.

There were some quite large poplar trees on this farm. Dad decided he would harvest some of them, take them to the sawmill, and use the lumber for some projects he had in mind. I don't remember whether I helped to fell the trees or not. I do remember helping saw them in lengths and load the logs on our farm trailer. We simply placed a couple of fairly long planks against the trailer, up which we rolled the logs. It was simple. We used cant hooks. They are devices that have a moderately long handle with a curved metal hook on one end that bites into the log and allows the logger to roll it wherever he wishes. The hook never gets caught. So we loaded the logs onto the trailer and transported them down to the McIntire farm where the sawmill was operating. The lumber was beautiful. When we brought the boards home, Dad made a major error in judgment. Usually, if not always, green lumber is stacked outside with strict attention to creating airflow space that will keep any part of it from rotting. It was early summer. The hay mows were empty. Dad thought it would be well to stack the boards there, pile hay on top, and let the hay pull the moisture out of the lumber. Of course, it did not work that way. The lumber did not dry properly, and most of it was lost. Dad was sick. And when Mother found out, he was even sicker. Mother was very committed to reminding Dad of his imperfections.

It was after Dad had been killed and Mother had moved to Circleville that Bill and I were at her house. We were trimming trees and doing anything else that needed attention around the property. Mother had prepared lunch for us. Mother was seated at the head of the table, and we boys on either side of her. She was talking about Dad. "We never had a cross word," she said.

My brother looked over at me and asked, "Were you born in the same house as I was?" Her statement was partly true. Dad seldom spoke back.

ROLLING HILLS

The last home butchering we did was on this farm. The object of our work on this day was a hog. We started the day before. A thirty-gallon drum was placed under a curly maple. A length of pipe was screwed into a receiving unit near the bottom of the drum. The drum was filled three-fourths of the way with water. Some wood was stacked along the pipe extending from the drum. Next morning a fire was kindled along the pipe. Every now and then there would be a kind of loud burp from the drum. The hot water was expanding in the line and circulating.

When all was ready, the pig was shot with a twenty-two-caliber rifle, and the jugular vein severed with a large butcher's knife so the animal's blood could flow out. Oh, I forgot, a rope and pulley apparatus had been secured to a limb of the maple. The carcass was pulled up over the drum of hot water, then lowered into the boiling liquid. It was dunked a few times until it was easy to scrape the hair off the skin. The carcass was then pulled up and the rope tied off. After the hair was fully removed from the skin, the carcass was gutted. After the gutting it was halved and hung in the barn to cool overnight.

The next day Dad cut the carcass up using a meat saw and butcher knives. This time the meat was wrapped in paper and placed in our freezer. In later years, the animals were taken to the Marietta Frozen Food Locker where they were killed, processed, and frozen. When the locker called, we went to town and picked up the packaged frozen meat. Sometimes Mother would say, "I am almost sure they kept some of the good cuts for themselves." Of course, that could never be proved. Upon reflection, Mother was fairly suspicious of other people's integrity. Maybe not a bad idea. Certainly not in our time.

Several processes used on the first farm were changed in the way we worked on this one. The thrashing machine gave way to the combine. Most years the Keller family from Watertown did that work. No gathering of community farmers to help. Just one or two men doing it all. There was no silo, so again, there was no gathering of community farmers to help with that task. Hay, after that first year or two, was baled, not put in the mow loose. Lime was sometimes spread by the truck that delivered it. We continued to milk cows and sell Grade B milk. Also, we continued to sell eggs and sometimes young chickens (and old ones too). I don't remember using the buck rake after the first year or two. And, of course, after Dad purchased our New Holland equipment, we baled everything, including the straw. I also baled for at least two neighbors who never paid us. One was a professing Christian? Professing is not necessarily possessing.

One winter night it snowed. It was snowing when we retired for the night. The snow kept coming down as we slept. I didn't know it, but Alvin Ford's little Ford coupe decided to act up and slide off the road into a ditch just below our house. My first awareness of this middle-of-the-night event was when a slat broke in the bed where Bill and I were sleeping. It was near daybreak. Alvin, one of Bill's closest friends, had come to the door after his auto mishap, and Mom had said, "Just go on in and get in bed with the boys." He did. It was not a king-sized, not even a queen-sized bed. I guess we were doing just fine until the slat had more weight than it could take, and down we went. No one went back to sleep after that. It wasn't long before someone was pounding on the front door. Alvin's car was partially blocking the state road. A supply truck needed to get through. There was some scurrying around. I think our Ford tractor would not start. So, Husky Worthington (his name was Harold, but he most always went by Husky) was summoned. He came with his Allis Chalmers, along with block and tackle. He soon had the car out of the ditch and traffic on its way.

Husky used his tractor another time I recall for the good of our local community. It was during the big snow of November 1950. That snow began falling on Thanksgiving Day and continued until Sunday morning. All roads in our area were blocked by snow drifts. Gene Morris and I had gone to Marietta on Saturday afternoon. Traffic was just about nonexistent. By the time we made it home, most every road was impassable. We were snowed in on Sunday, Monday, and Tuesday. On Wednesday morning Husky came up and said he planned to see if he could get the road opened to Barlow and asked if we would help. So after lunch we began the trek with several neighbors.

Husky went ahead of us on the Allis Chalmers. He would cut a track in the snow, and where it was too deep for a car to move, we would shovel it away. Many areas were already clear. The wind had taken care of that. The problem was that in some places the snow was drifted up to a depth of four feet or more. In those places we shoveled for a good spell. Finally by four or so in the afternoon, we made it the two and a half miles to Barlow. The urgency, according to Husky, was because there was a pregnant woman or two out our way who might need to be transported to the hospital in Marietta. What I didn't know at the time, was that Mr. W. H. Heiby, for whom I would later work, had brought his bulldozer out Route A-50 to help clear that road. The operator told me a year or two later, when I worked for the company, that they had a bottle of good whiskey with them to keep them warm.

My brother and his wife were, at that time, home from Trevecca Nazarene College in Nashville, Tennessee. They left on Thursday morning with chains on their car. They later told us the chains were removed at Athens. The roads were mostly clear from there on to Tennessee. Interesting that the snow was so deep in our community, but fifteen miles away the roads were almost clear. I know the Bible indicates that "It rains on the just and on the unjust." I suppose it is the same with snow. Who was who in that situation?

In 1950 I was the proud owner of a Model A Ford. Sometime after the road to Barlow was opened, I felt compelled to go see Betty Maze. I was able to get as far as Rocky Point Hill. For the next mile or so, the road was drifted shut. I turned the old car around, headed it back down the hill, shut it off, set the brake, and headed the three-quarters of a mile for the Maze house. The road in some places was totally blocked by snow

THE SECOND FARM AND MY TEENAGE YEARS

drifts, so I walked up on the road bank as much as possible. It was quite an adventure, but I made it to the door and was warmly welcomed. Going back to the old car seemed more challenging. I, however, made it, and the old vehicle started. When one is in love there are few challenges that are strong enough to prevent a rendezvous.

Later, Dad and Mom bought me a 1939 Dodge sedan. It was a nice car for a high school junior. It served me well. There are at least two events that happened with that vehicle that are worth recalling. First, one night I had been out quite late. It was a Saturday. During my trip back to our farmhouse, I must have fallen asleep. All I remember is that I was awakened by the car shaking and bouncing around. I was running fifty miles an hour along a fence, high on the road bank. Quickly I steered the car back onto the road. I arrived home safe and sound. The next afternoon I decided to go back and see just where I had been. I had missed a concrete culvert by just a few feet. Had I hit that immovable object, it is hard to imagine how many injuries I would have been dealt.

It was that car that I drove to Nashville, Tennessee a few times. On one trip to Nashville it blew a piston ring and cost one hundred dollars to repair. The problem was the result of being a good Samaritan. A man and his wife had asked me to take them to Nashville, when I returned following Christmas break. When I went to Belpre to pick them up, they had a huge trunk that was far too heavy for this car plus the passengers. I finally pushed the trunk into the car and tied down the trunk lid. We headed south. I noticed a miss in the engine sometime before we entered the city of Nashville. It was bad news.

The couple who had asked me to transport them to Nashville had a baby with them. Somewhere in the hills of Kentucky the baby became hungry. Finally, the father of the child directed me to stop at a house along the road so he could try to persuade the owner to warm the baby's milk. He took the bottle with him, knocked on the door, the door opened, and he disappeared from sight. His wife, the crying baby, and I waited in the car. And we waited some more. Nearly an hour. Finally, the father came out with some warm milk. His wife, a bit exasperated, asked him why it took so long. His reply was, "The man had to build a fire in the stove, wait for it to heat, and when the stove had warmed up enough, he heated the milk." He didn't seem to think anything about our waiting.

I was graduated from Vincent High School in May 1951 and went to work for The W. H. Heiby Company later that month. That job came about one Friday afternoon when I was hanging out on Putman Street in Marietta. I looked up and saw Husky Worthington coming toward me. He greeted me by asking, "Do you want to go to work?" I told him I did. He invited me to walk with him up the street to the Colony Theater. He introduced me to Orton Wallace, who was a foreman for the company. They were completing repair work on that building and were about to go to work on the Putman Theater just across the street. Heiby Company was repairing the roof of the Putman. My directive was to be there at 8:00 a.m. on Monday morning.

I was on time and was working when one of the owners, Mr. Harry Hudson, came up to look things over. I had met him at the Colony job when I was hired. As he approached, I greeted him, "Good morning Mr. Hudson." He walked on past me without a word. A little later he came by and said, "Good morning, Hill, how is it going?" I reminded him that I had greeted him some minutes before. "Oh," he said, "I must have had my mind on some matter and didn't hear." He was a good man. Could be humorous.

Mr. Hudson probably drank more than he should have. He was taking me someplace one afternoon to load construction items on his company truck. He told me that he had taken his wife to her hair appointment late that morning. He said he sat in the truck and waited for her. When she came out, he received a word of gratitude from her. "Harry it is so good of you," she said, "to sit and wait for me instead of running off to some bar." He said, "I thanked her, but she didn't know I was already so 'tight' I could hardly sit still."

I liked construction work and stayed with it until I left in late August 1951 for Nashville, Tennessee. There I lived with Bill and Kathryn, my brother and his wife, from August until the following May. During the day I worked first at a Texaco station on Murfreesboro Pike and later for the Pamplin Distributing Co. At the latter job I delivered auto parts and accessories throughout the area. At night I attended Ball's School of Technology. It was my plan to pursue life as an automobile mechanic.

I experienced many life-maturing events while living in the city of Nashville. At Ball's School of Technology, where I studied auto mechanics, I learned how to rebuild engines, gear trains, electrical systems, and more. Diesel engines and how they functioned were also part of the course. One student I met there was from Cuba. He was a rather unhinged young fellow, but very likeable. I have often wondered what happened to him when Castro took over.

One night when I was working in live engines, some of us engaged in some really stupid behavior. These engines were mounted on stands so the whole unit was available for visual instruction. On this particular night, three or four of us were standing around a V-8 engine. Someone raised the question as to whether we could kill the engine by spreading our hands across the spark plug connections, grasping them tightly, thus grounding the electrical charge, and stopping the unit. Of course, we had to try it. To my surprise, my hands with fingers fully extended could touch all the plugs on a V-8 as I stood in front of it. I killed the engine. I killed it a number of times. Only later would I learn that such behavior could negatively affect the heart. Might even have killed us. It seems for some it takes a long time for wisdom to take root and grow.

While I was living in Nashville, I experienced segregation up close and personal. The first day I was going downtown to take a look around. I decided to ride the bus instead of driving my car. I wanted to get the feel of things. When I boarded the bus, it was nearly empty. There was one, maybe two people in the very back seat. So, being a kind of humble young man, I sat in the second seat from the front. As the bus rumbled along, I was aware of it stopping and taking on passengers, but I was so preoccupied with drinking in the city sites that I was also unconscious of all that was happening within the vehicle. While I was very preoccupied with the activity outside, someone approached me and asked me if I would move up so he could sit down. I was shocked, but quickly moved up to the front seat. When I looked around, it was clear. I was the only white person on the bus. And the rule was, "White to the front, Negros to the back." My first real introduction to segregation in the United States of America.

Mr. Pamplin, my boss, took me to lunch one day when I was working for him. The restaurant had two entrances, side by side. The door on the right was labeled "White." The one on the left, "Negro." We entered through the one for white folks. As I remember it, the two sections were separated by some kind of screening. Each side could see the other. As I sat there, I pondered the rules. I could be a person of very limited use in that society, but if I were white, then some special attention was focused on me. On the other hand, if I were a Negro doctor who specialized in saving lives, I was sent to the other side where the second-class citizens were required to go. Someone had to keep me in my place. There truly was something wrong with this setup. Yet, even today there are some folks who think segregation was the best arrangement and would return this land to it if they could.

The segregation rules hit me directly between the eyes one night when I was coming back to Nashville on a Trailways Bus. I am no longer certain of just how the family secured my name, but I received a call wondering if I would drive an elderly man down to his summer home in Water Valley, Mississippi. There was a small stipend offered. I agreed to do it. I can remember yet, as we hit the Mississippi state line, the gentleman said, "Now whenever I come to this place, I usually set it on seventy-five and leave it there. The road is perfectly straight for the next ten miles." It was a fairly new Pontiac straight-8. I put the pedal to the metal and let her sing at seventy-five miles an hour. Heady stuff for an eighteen-year-old.

Once we arrived at his house about 3:00 p.m. he said, "Now I will buy you a ticket back to Nashville or give you twenty dollars if you want to hitchhike." I had observed, as we drove along during the afternoon, the long stretches of highway running through miles of swamp. I had no desire to be out there alone at night, hoping for a ride as the guest of whoever might pick me up. I took the ticket. The young woman at the bus station was very caring. She truly wanted me to be comfortable. She even walked with me to the bus and wished me well. She kind of acted like she would go with me if I asked. I guess it was just southern hospitality.

Somewhere in upstate Mississippi, long after dark, we made a pit stop. The driver said, "There is a washroom here if you need one, and a little restaurant if you would like a sandwich." Well, I made use of the washroom and headed for the hamburger joint. I was served quickly and came back outside where the bus was parked. The driver was talking to two young black men who were impeccably dressed in United States Air Force uniforms. These men had been in the back of the bus, of course, therefore I had not seen them. No way could they sit up near where my skin allowed me to be. The driver was saying to these two handsome, clean-cut, uniformed US Servicemen, "The man said that he would sell you some sandwiches if you will go around to the back door." This was the spring of 1952. The Korean War was still in progress, and these soldiers were told, "If you want something to eat, go to the back door and the man will take your money there." And I wondered to myself, *If this is segregation, what did slavery look like?*

There was a lesson in American justice that I learned one night while working on some part of an automobile. The man speaking, I will call Wally (not his real name). He was tall, had a southern drawl, and was quite focused. He had been overseas for a couple of years or more. He came home and moved into an apartment with his wife. After a few days, the owner of the apartment confronted him. "Why are you living with that other man's wife?" he asked.

Wally was shocked. "This is my wife; we have been married for several years," he said. The apartment owner said no more. He probably knew he had said too much already.

In a few weeks, Wally's wife told him she was with child. Remembering what the landlord had said, he was even more surprised that she was at least three months pregnant. He filed for divorce, and it was granted. There was, however, one problem. Wally was partially disabled due to the war, and he was receiving a pension. He had spent several weeks in a military hospital before being mustered out. Support for this child was subtracted from his pension benefits. He would have to support the child until she was eighteen. Wally was one unhappy man about that. Most of us would be as well. Justice is sometimes truly blind.

There is one final Nashville story I wish to share before I move on. Ball's School of Technology was designed for veterans. There were, however, quite a number of us who had not served our country in that way. School began in late evening and ran to 11:00 p.m. I was still driving my 1939 Dodge four-door. Being young and sometimes thoughtless, I didn't worry much about anything. Yet, on the night of this event, I had, when I entered the car to drive home, locked all four doors. The route I followed took me over the Cumberland River. On the downtown Nashville side of the bridge, there were stoplights. I was about half asleep, probably smoking a cigarette, maybe daydreaming about something as I came down the approach. Suddenly the lights turned red, and I came to a quick stop.

Just as I stopped the car, four older youths came quickly to the car. Each one grabbed a door handle. They tried desperately to get in. Yes, one was even yanking on the driver's side door and looking me directly in the face as I was looking at him. But because the doors were locked, the boys failed to complete their mission. I have often wondered what would

THE SECOND FARM AND MY TEENAGE YEARS

have happened had they been able to open those doors. In a split second I hit the gas, let the clutch out, and ran the red light. Life is a wonderful adventure, but it can be dangerous. Looking back, I have escaped many life-threating moments.

The last night in Nashville I did a bit of partying and drove out of town after midnight. I had decided to go to Pikeville, Kentucky, and visit my Uncle Charles, Mother's brother, and Aunt Lillian, his second wife. For some reason I felt adventurous, so I took a very secondary road at one point. The map indicated that I would have to take a ferry across some river. I thought that would be just great. As I drove along this road, I think it was Route 300, a very narrow path, I came around a turn in the road, and there up close and personal were three or four men, mountain men, nearly blocking the road with their car. I took a deep breath, waved at them, and slowly made my way forward with the left-side wheels in a shallow road ditch. None of them moved. A few miles later I came to the river. Shock! The ferry wasn't running. There had been a hard rain, and the water was too swift and high. What was I to do? There was only one real solution—turn around, retrace my tracks past the mountain men, and continue on the better road, even though it would take longer. Surprise! (Again!) When I came to where the men had been, they were gone. I exhaled heartily.

I spent the night with Uncle Charlie and Aunt Lillian just outside of Pikeville, Kentucky. Uncle told me a story I still remember. He was a driller. He came to the drilling platform one night, and the man he was relieving asked if he had been over in Harlan earlier that day. "Yes," my uncle responded. The man then told him, "You were lucky to get out of there. Someone took you for a federal revenuer and was about to take care of you. But a man who was present said, 'No, he is all right. He helped me with my car a few days ago.'"

Uncle told me that he had come upon a man who was having car trouble. He stopped and asked if there was a problem. The man told him that his car wouldn't start. He had stopped on the roadside for some reason, and when he got back in, the car was dead. Uncle asked if it was all right for him to look under the hood. The man said it was. My uncle found a battery terminal clamp loose and corroded. He retrieved his tools from the trunk of his car, took the connection off, scraped all surfaces with his pocketknife, then replaced and tightened the clamp. The car started immediately. The man went on his way. He thought nothing about it until the driller friend told him how close he had come to harm. A good deed can sometimes be worth its weight in gold. It is helpful to remember the Golden Rule, "Do to others as you would have others do to you."

The next morning I headed toward Charleston, West Virginia. This, of course, was years before the interstate freeways. There were three or four mountains to be crossed before I reached West Virginia's capitol city. That drive in itself was an adventure. On the way to Charleston, however, I picked up a hitchhiker. It was something I did without thinking. Just stopped and said, "Get in." As we drove along, I began to think, *This guy could kill me, throw my body over one of these precipices, and no one would ever know.* I grew more and more uncomfortable, but there was nothing I could do. He was bigger than me. I worked at keeping a relaxed countenance. And in the end, everything turned out all right. As we approached a certain crossroads, he said, "This is where I need to get out." He thanked me for the ride, and I went on my way. Not every person is out to harm us, but how do we discern the good from the dangerous?

That is a question that is on my mind today as I observe some very serious believers who seek to establish a Christian nationalist government right here in the United States. They say it is important for all our laws to be based on an infallible interpretation of the Bible. That means for many, that there would be no mixing of races and no women in places of leadership. Women, in all categories, would be subservient to men, for that is this group's interpretation of scripture. Too, only Christian schools would

THE SECOND FARM AND MY TEENAGE YEARS

be allowed, and all social relationships would be controlled by Biblical edicts and enforced by a US, biblically authorized virtue police.

This theological understanding is the reason why many evangelical Christians supported Donald Trump for President of the United States. They hoped that he would work with them to establish a theocracy in this land. Of course, these believers embrace a multitude of conflicting scriptural understandings. That one fact alone would lead to constant bedlam. The Church should have major influence over its members and should inform any candidate for membership about what is expected. But the Constitution of the United States is the only touchstone for all that is political and secular. And yes, every church should be free to practice their beliefs freely in our secular society, so long as they do not try to pass laws that call for citizens to be controlled by their biblically based doctrines. One person's faith is his or her own business, but should that person seek to force their beliefs on others by politically passing laws to enforce those beliefs, it would be destructive. That is certainly one reason our forefathers created a nation where Church and State are supposed to be separate.

My training in Nashville taught me to understand the way gasoline and diesel engines function and how to repair them. I also learned some about gear trains and electrical systems. There was a national steel strike on, however, in May of 1952 when I returned to Ohio. Work was not easy to find, so I overhauled our Ford tractor. The work was successful. The tractor had new power, and Dad thought I was a genius.

I applied for a job, among other places, at Williamson Chevrolet in Beverly. I heard nothing from that company. After waiting for several weeks, I had an opportunity to return to the Heiby Company, and I took it. The Chevrolet company called me the day after I began with Heiby. I stayed with the company I knew. I worked for them for quite some time and then joined the Carpenters Union. Later I worked for another company that was building a new plant down along the Ohio River between Marietta and Belpre. I still remember the afternoon the paymaster brought my final check. It had a slip in it telling me my services were no longer needed. When I saw it, my response was, "This is the last pink slip I will receive from construction. My life has to be more secure than this." And that was the last time I was laid off.

A few of the projects I worked on in the Marietta Area while in the employ of the Heiby Company stand out in my mind: the riverboat addition to the Campus Martius Museum, the YMCA building near the old high school, installing new equipment at the B. F. Goodrich Company up the river from the city, elevator shafts at Remington Rand, hauling used brick for a few, special, high-dollar houses being constructed on Water Works Hill, a new subdivision on Harmer Hill, and the first unit of the new Warren School Building. The new subdivision on Harmer Hill took a lot of time. I began there as the chain guy for the surveyor. A farm was sacrificed for a new housing development.

I also helped to seed the lawn at a new grade school nearby. Mr. Edwards, one of the Heiby Company big bosses, came to our work shack one morning and said, "Hill, I need you to come over to the schoolhouse with me for a little while today."

Knowing that Mr. Edwards sometime treated time a bit strangely, I asked, "Shall I bring my lunch bucket?"

He stood and thought about it for at least twenty seconds and replied, "Oh, bring it. You may not be back here in time for lunch." I stayed at the school for at least two weeks. I worked with those preparing the lawn.

It was in that setting one day that the cement finishers who were working on the sidewalks ate lunch with me and a few other men. We began to talk about ages. "How old do you think I am?" one of the cement finishers asked. I looked at him for a good long time. His hair to me was white. I did not want to be too far off the mark, so I guessed him to be sixty-eight. He was forty-eight. He looked really hurt. I regretted my guess. From that day on I never again indulged in the age-guessing game.

Later in that subdivision I helped set up a Gunnison house. These

THE SECOND FARM AND MY TEENAGE YEARS

were prefabricated units. On the morning of the house raising when we arrived on the jobsite, there was a tractor trailer sitting near the foundation. The house was on the truck, in pieces. The foundation and subfloor had been completed sometime before. We began to unload the pieces and carry them over to the team on the subfloor. At the end of the day, the house was up. It would take a few weeks for the finish work to be completed. I believe all the houses in that complex were Gunnisons. As I checked the spelling for this product just now on the internet, it appears that the size, quality, and price have expanded. Just saw a Gunnison on the market in Colorado for $759,000. In 1952 the ones we were building may have been selling for about $18,000. They were quite small, but very adequate for young couples who truly wanted a place of their own, a place that would gain in value as time passed. Some of those houses are now probably worth close to $100,000.

When I started on the Warren School building job, my category was hod carrier. That means I was a common laborer and spent my time carrying concrete blocks or mortar. And after a few days of carrying twelve-inch blocks, it was clear to me that being a carpenter would be a step up. So I spoke to some people, joined the Carpenters and Joiners Union, and began to work as an apprentice carpenter.

My very first day as an apprentice carpenter, I was assigned to nailing down gymnasium subfloor. By the end of the day, my left hand began to look like a war casualty. It takes a lot of energy to swing a hammer for eight hours. After a few hours, my right arm and wrist became hard to control. I couldn't tell just where the hammer would land when I dropped it. Even though I had a glove on my left hand, that extremity was bruised and battered. After a few days, however, my arm strengthened and things went better.

As the work at Warren School came to a close, I was sent to a new plant down the river from Marietta. I cannot remember how long I was there. But I endured a strike or two and was laid off in late summer.

ROLLING HILLS

After being laid off I made up my mind to find another approach to life. A few months later I was hired by the Goodyear Atomic Corporation. That company had the contract to build and operate the Atomic Gaseous Diffusion Plant near Piketon. I became a process operator and thought I had found the place from which I would retire. Life, however, packs a lot of surprises, good and not so good. I was about to be surprised once more.

CHAPTER 15

THE DECISION OF A LIFETIME

IN MAY OF 1952, when I arrived back in Washington County, Ohio, from Nashville, Tennessee, I moved into my old room at Mom and Dad's farmhouse. I helped with chores and other farm work. And as stated previously, I went back to the Heiby Company. Betty Maze and I also continued our romance. Yet it seems we had drifted apart while I was away, and gradually our relationship fell apart. She became engaged to someone else, a fine young fellow who was a bit older. With my work on construction and on the farm, there wasn't a whole lot of free time. I did not find another girlfriend and thus was kind of at loose ends.

Then one Saturday evening in early September, Dad and I, with the help of a couple of boys from Vincent, were baling hay and storing it in the barn. The hay was some kind of lespedeza. It may have been a third cutting, for it grew rapidly. We had a load or two of bales left in the field when we broke for supper. We were bringing in the last load, sometime around eight o'clock. While I was maneuvering the tractor and farm trailer for the process of backing the load into the upper part of the barn, out the corner of one eye, I observed Mother and someone sitting in the front porch swing. I didn't think much about it. But after we had completed the work and I had put trailer and tractor away until needed again, my curiosity became too much. I made my way to the front side of the house to see who was there.

The person sitting with Mother was Betty Maze. She was wearing a red dress with white polka dots. She was beautiful. We greeted each other rather causally and engaged, I suppose, in some small talk. I don't remember whether she had her diamond on that night or not. I have a feeling she didn't. After a little while I realized that there was no car in the parking area. "How did you get here?" I asked. She told me that someone had brought her. After all these years, I do not remember who it was who brought her, and if she does, she is not telling.

"How do you plan to get home?" I inquired.

"I thought you might take me," she said with a smile that would have melted ice. Reflecting now on that moment, I cannot recall what all went through my mind. I did, however, tell her that it would take some time to bathe and get dressed. I would then take her home.

In many ways that evening sealed our fate, and in February of 1953, we were married. That was sixty-nine years ago. There have been great times and not so great times, like with all marriages. But after all these years, we are parents of four wonderful daughters, four grandchildren, and at this writing, seven great-grandchildren. And we all love each other and care deeply about each other's welfare.

Sometime during the summer of 1952, I overhauled my 1946 Ford. Yes, I had traded the Dodge for the Ford, with a little help from Mom and Dad. It was a six-cylinder. It was a Saturday night, and I was racing to finish the job. I was to pick Betty up at the Blennerhassett Restaurant in Belpre at midnight when the place closed. As I was busy tightening the pan bolts, Bill Meek walked onto the barn floor where I was working. He said something to me, and I automatically tried to answer. The problem was I had a mouthful of tobacco juice. At that time, I was a smoker. But because I was in the barn, that wasn't an option. So I had purchased a package of Red Man and had some of it in my mouth. Forgetting the situation, I attempted to answer Bill. I was somewhat successful, but in the process, swallowed most of that horrible stuff that was in my mouth. I came out from under the car and ejected the rest of that despicable elixir. It makes me half sick now just to think about it. That was the last time I had chewing tobacco in my mouth. And to this day I have not missed it. Never liked it anyway. One wonders why I would have done it in the first place. I can say that about a number of behaviors I embraced from time to time across the years.

In 1953 I was selling Guardian Service Cookware. I got a call from Mr. Edwards at the Heiby Company. He said they had a few days of work for me. I thought for a moment and told him to give it to someone else. (Looking back, had I taken that few days, it might have lengthened into years, for Mr. Edwards had a strange sense of time, as I've stated previously.) I knew, however, that before we started a family, I needed a job that would sustain us.

In the summer of 1954, I put in an application to the Goodyear Atomic Corp in Piketon, Ohio. In early December of that year, I went to work there. The FBI checked me out. A representative went back to Palmer and asked about my background. They checked my stay in Waterford, and probably reviewed whether I had any criminal record. I still remember one of the questions put to me before I received my Q clearance: "Why have you moved around so much?"

Whatever my response was, it must have been OK. Mostly my task was to read systems pressures, act busy on dayshift, and try not to be bored. Midnight to eight in the morning was always challenging. Some days I hardly knew whether I was getting up or going to bed. In fact we all carried cards showing us when we should report for work. We swung every seven days. The final months of my employment there I was assigned to Product Withdrawal. That plant's product was transported to Oak Ridge, Tennessee, for further refinement.

I mentioned my Q clearance. That status allowed me to enter any part of the plant where I was required to work. And to be honest, it did not allow me to know anything that was not paramount to my work responsibility. In fact, we were reminded again and again, "You will be told what you need to know." In these days, as I hear all about what special secrets QAnon has uncovered with his or her "Q clearance," I just don't attach any validity to the conspiracies attributed to the Anonymous One. It is fake all the way, in my opinion. Even Q (if he/she exists) knows only what he/she is told by the powers who are above.

The first several months while I was working at Piketon, Betty stayed with my parents while I lived in Beaver, Ohio. I came home on every break from work. But after our first child, Anita, was born in September of 1955, we knew it was important to be together as a family. I looked at a house not far from Wellston, but it was not what we wanted—wood and coal heating stove and outdoor privy. One day we learned that the mobile home we had rented from Mr. Victor Underwood for a couple of years while Betty was working as a waitress at his restaurant was for sale. We contacted him and purchased it.

The Underwood family were great people. Mr. Underwood told me one night that when the 1929 depression hit, he owned a restaurant in the area and lost everything. "But," he said, "just as soon as the recovery began and I could find a place to borrow money, I started again." He ran a good restaurant and sustained a very profitable business until he sold out in the late 1950s. I can remember stopping at the restaurant one evening after it had been taken over by the new owners. Prices had gone up. A hamburger was fifty cents. I thought the price was totally unreasonable. They had been twenty-five cents or a little more. Now a hamburger with chips is around ten dollars. Times have changed.

It cost us thirty-eight dollars to hire a man to move our mobile home from Rockland, Ohio, to Pike County. I cannot believe it! Financial life was truly different then.

THE DECISION OF A LIFETIME

Before we brought the mobile home to Pike County, I had lived the first two weeks with Uncle Robert, one of Mother's brothers, at Hamden, Ohio. Uncle was working construction at the plant. Next, I moved to a rooming house in Beaver. Four of us men stayed in one very large room. Ray Simmons, a construction worker, was living in the same rooming house. In fact, Ray was the one who told me that there was an open bed there. Later, Ray found an old farmhouse outside of Beaver, and together we four men rented it. Ray did the cooking, and the rest of us did the cleaning. We all shared the expenses. That arrangement worked well for us.

One major memory of that experience happened on a rainy spring night. Just how this series of stupidities unfolded I don't recall. I locked the keys in my 1988 Oldsmobile with lights on and the engine running. With some farmer ingenuity I was, after a lot of frustration and failure, able to use a coat hanger, reach in and unlock the door. Great! But within a half an hour I did the same thing again. Where was my mind? Probably trying to figure out when I was scheduled to work again. The second time, however, took very little work. By that time I knew exactly how to undo my mistake. "Practice makes perfect," someone once said. I suppose that also helps explain why I locked the door with the lights on and engine running the second time.

With all that behind me, Betty, the baby, and I located our mobile home just a mile from Givens Station in Pike County. Givens Station may no longer be on the map, but it was within a thirty-minute drive to the atomic plant. Those were some very good times. But after a couple of years, we purchased a large lot in Beaver that already had water and sewer hookup installed on it. A Mrs. Little, who had lived near us at Givens Station, moved her mobile home onto our lot and paid rent. I built a small utility building on the east side of the mobile home for storage and room for a washing machine. Life there was good.

Looking back, I wonder if our becoming involved with the Beaver Methodist Church was a motivating factor in that move. We had become deeply involved with that congregation. We had attended Sunday school and worship a time or two when there was a request for volunteer drivers to transport youth to a special gathering. I volunteered to drive. A short time after that event, the pastor, Rev. Roy Locher, and his wife visited us at our home. It was a Sunday afternoon, October 30, 1955. I was not working that weekend. Rev. and Mrs. Locher urged us to come to church that night. After a long resistance, I agreed to be there. I really didn't want to go, but I had promised. Remember, I am an ISTJ. That commitment was not negotiable. There were fourteen people present. Rev. Roy Locher was a real evangelical. He had been Pilgrim Holiness educated. When the altar call was given, after a short argument with myself, I went forward and surrendered my life to Christ, so far as I knew how. Betty was soon by my side.

The major force in my decision to re-embrace the church was the birth of our first child. As I held her in my arms and saw how fragile she was, it dawned upon me that she would need a lot of care and nurturing. And furthermore, what she grew to become in this life would be greatly shaped by how her parents brought her up, especially how we related to her. The job of parenting looked larger than any task I had ever faced. So I needed help, and I moved to God and the church to find it.

The following Sunday was World Wide Communion Day. That Sunday the full ritual found in the 1939 Methodist Hymnal was used. There was a lot of confessing how low-down every human being is. I would not read the words. I had been "saved," and now I was "perfect." It took a little while for me to realize that being a Christian required more than going forward, kneeling, confessing, and being "saved." I learned that I could still act like a sinner. So the long journey toward reflecting the spirit of Jesus in my life began.

I am still trying to reach that "perfection" of which Wesley spoke. I'm not there yet. It was in seminary that I began to understand more fully the miracle of God's grace. It's not about us. It is about That Something

More, whom we call God, but who has many names. That Force gives us life whether we deserve it or not. It is up to us to use it for good. To "Treat others as we wish to be treated." Or, more theologically sound, "To treat others as God has treated us."

I didn't know it at the time, but that trip to the chancel rail at the Beaver Methodist Church on an October evening in 1955 would change my life and Betty's life forever. It would also determine much about the milieu in which my family and I would live in the coming years. As Betty and I became active in that local church, I gradually felt the call of God upon my life to enter Christian ministry. Reverend Roy Locher saw something in me that caused him to support and nudge me toward Christian service.

Others in the church played a major role in nurturing me in the faith as well. After Sunday school one morning, Henry Stoll and Jim Hoover, both really good men, came to me and said they had concluded that I should become the teacher of the men's class. I had been attending that group for several months. Mr. Stoll had been teaching the class for forty years. (He and his wife Hattie were our lay members to Annual Conference for years.) I didn't feel capable of such a task and told them so. But Henry, a good and gracious man, said, "I will be there every Sunday, and I will help you." He was, and he did. Thank you, Henry.

Often, when one has been a leader for a long time, even in church, that person will fight to keep their job. But here was a man who wanted to help a young person learn more. He was a prince of a man. I taught the class and accepted other jobs in that church. The good pastor invited me to preach for him one Sunday evening, June 9, 1956. As I write these words, the faded manuscript used that night lies before me. The title was "Following Christ." The text was Matthew 9:9. My father was in the congregation that night. He told my mother, "He preached a lot like Grandpa Nutter." I think that meant I was quite animated. It was a beginning. Later I preached for Rev. Locher at the Savageville Church.

In June of 1958 I was sent, as a student pastor, to The Rodney Charge of the Methodist Church. It was made up of five rural congregations: Rodney, Cora, Alexander, Centenary, and Fairfield. Combined membership on this circuit was 191. Total salary paid was $2,600. In early spring 1958, I had met the Board of Ministerial Training in the parlor of Maple Grove Church, located at Henderson and High Streets in Columbus, Ohio. I remember only one question that was put to me: "How do you plan to live on the salary you'll receive as a student pastor?" That question was put to me by Reverend Nobel Rompel. He was pastor of Maple Grove at the time. My response was, "I have faith to believe that God will take care of me and my family." Rompel kind of shook his head and asked no more questions.

My assigned task was to pastor those five small membership congregations and attend Rio Grande College (now University of Rio Grande) at the same time. Those years added greatly to my knowledge, not only academically, but also how church management looks from the inside. Our sojourn in Rio Grande was four years in length. It was a major learning experience. Not only did Miss Clara Poston help me understand grammar, Reverend Luther Tracy guided me through some very helpful Bible courses. Too, Mrs. Zelma Northcutt was a great help with music. I became a member of the college choir for a year or two. R.P. Ewing taught literature. He was special.

Bevo Francis helped Rio Grande gain national attention several years before I became a student there. The college had an outstanding basketball team for a short time. Bevo was the star. He set many records that have not been broken. R.P. Ewing once stated in class, "Bevo didn't help much with the student morale of the school, for everyone knew we were giving him passing grades, even though he didn't deserve them. But it was kind of nice," he said with a smile, "to beat Miami of Florida."

I was graduated from Rio Grande in May 1962. It was time to move on. While at Rio Grande we added another member to the family. We named her Elizabeth. She was our third daughter. Barbara was born before we left Beaver and the Goodyear Company to head into ministry.

In June of 1962, my family and I moved to Derby Charge in Pickaway County. We were appointed to a three-point circuit this time: Derby, Greenland, and Five Points. We served those congregations for three years while I attended classes at The Methodist Theological School in Delaware, Ohio. At the Twentieth Session of the Ohio Annual Conference, held at Lakeside, Ohio, I was ordained deacon by Bishop Hazen G. Werner. Betty was not with me at that time, for she was with child. But my mother, a lay member from the Vincent Church, was present and stood behind me on that ninth day of June, 1963, as Bishop Hazen Werner ordained me a deacon in The Methodist Church.

That moment suddenly came to mind many years later in 1994, when, as District Superintendent, I was attending the Annual Conference at Lakeside. We were celebrating the Holy Eucharist in Hoover Auditorium. That sacred place was at capacity, and it seats 3,000. As I was distributing the bread and wine to the delegates at one station, it suddenly hit me that I was now standing within a few feet of where I was made a deacon in the Methodist Church many years before when Mother was still alive and standing beside me. She had died just a few weeks earlier at the age of ninety-four. Suddenly, emotion that I did not realize was within me let go. Bishop Judith Craig, who was in charge, told me she saw tears running down my face and wondered what was happening to me. I told her, then I said that Mother had been ill for so long I thought I had done my grief work. She said, "Charles, you know better, you can't do your grief work until the loss is real." Bishop Craig was very special to all of us who worked with her.

My Ordination for Elders Orders was held in the Lockbourne Methodist Church, October 2, 1966. The Elders Ordination gave me authority to serve pastoral or administrative positions anywhere in the Methodist Denomination. Following our three years serving the South

Bloomfield Circuit, we were moved to Jeffersonville in Fayette County, then to Hilliard United Methodist in Franklin County. (A merger with the Evangelical United Brethren Church took place in 1968 while we were serving at Jeffersonville, and the above name was chosen for the new denomination.) Following the thirteen Hilliard years, we were sent to Maple Grove UMC located at Henderson and High Streets in Columbus, Ohio, the intersection where there are an abundant number of auto accidents annually, sometimes daily.

In August of 1992, I was appointed Superintendent of the Springfield District. We retired in 1998 and then served Yellow Springs UMC from 2002 to 2010. Later, at the request of our district superintendent, we served two small membership country churches for a while, Brighton and Pitchin. As I recall it, the request was for a couple of months, but we stayed about two years. My plan is to, in the near future, share in a book some of our experiences as we pastored the above-named congregations and the district. So, stay tuned.

CHAPTER 16

REFLECTIONS

AS I HAVE LOOKED BACK across the early years of my life, it is quite clear to me that there is much for which to be grateful. First, Mom and Dad maintained a stable household. We boys learned early in life what the rules of the family were. These rules did not change from hour to hour or day to day. On occasion the rules may have been tweaked a bit, but not much or often.

Second, we learned that it was not all about any one of us. Each of us belonged to a family, something larger than ourselves. That may, on occasion, have been a challenge to grasp. I can remember a few times when I was feeling deprived, whining about not getting all that I wanted. Mother would say, "Nobody likes me, everybody hates me, I'm going to the garden to eat worms." Usually, those words reminded me that I was not as bad off as I perceived. Sometimes they even made me laugh and caused me to join the human race again.

Third, as I grew in understanding, I realized that there were family members who did not live in our house. There were grandparents and cousins—Mother being one of seventeen children, I had cousins by the dozen. At family reunions on occasion in the early years, there were more than two hundred of these other family members in attendance. Yes, I really was a part of something big. I remember one Nutter family reunion down in West Virginia, in the pines near a branch of Hughes' River, when a piano was brought in on a flatbed truck, and we shared in a worship service after the great dinner we all enjoyed. Uncle Carl Nutter, radio evangelist, preached. I was a teenager at the time. I think I didn't pay much attention to that service. May God forgive me. In fact, on one of those reunion days, Paul Beckner and I went joyriding with a couple of girls. I think the one with me was maybe a third cousin. She was redheaded. She sang some hillbilly songs. She was in tune, but I thought her voice was harsh. Oh well, it was just for a little while on a Sunday afternoon. Never saw her again.

The Hill family reunions were large in my early years, too. Sometimes that group would number more than two hundred. But the Hills were more introverted than the Nutter family. I do not remember any singing. Nor was there a lot of laughter. Everyone was friendly, but in a very subdued and quiet manner. In my adult years, as the group grew smaller, my brother sang on a regular basis. One or two years I sang with him. We are both tenors. But it was still a very quiet gathering.

Too, there was the school. In that venue I was pushed into relationships with children who were like me, yet different. I remember one day at Palmer Elementary a new boy came. I was in the fifth grade and so was he. He was dressed in clothing much better than most of us wore. But he cried all the time. I later learned that he was a foster child. As I remember it, he came only the one day. I never knew the full story. He was hurting in ways that none of us could have imagined. I hope he received the help and love he was missing.

At that grade school I came in contact with Black children. In those days they were called "Negroes." Palmer was not far from the Cutler Community. That place had been a stop on the Underground Railroad.

Too, there were bright and not-so-bright children with whom I was in contact. My eyes were opened to a more diverse world. I was a part of something very large with a multitude of variations.

One girl, who was a year or two ahead of me at Palmer Elementary, looked quite different. Someone, maybe my mother, shared with me the fact that she looked different because she had a harelip. It was quite a handicap. The condition made speaking clearly quite difficult. One day she was not present. I believe Miss Goddard was the teacher at that time, and she told us all that this girl would be out of class for a while. She was going to Columbus to have some surgery so she could speak more clearly. When she returned, not only did she speak more clearly, she looked different too. I am sure the medical attention she received changed her life dramatically. Now she looked like all the rest of us. When we are young, belonging is super important.

Finally, there was the church. There I learned that I was a part of something that had (in some form) been around for two thousand years. I not only belonged to a family with parents, brothers, grandparents, cousins, and more, a family with various kinds of countenances and skills, I also belonged to the family of God. All of that acceptance affirmed the fact that I am all right. I have a right to be here. "I am somebody," as Jesse Jackson reminded so many young Black youth across the years.

My experiences with others have helped make me who I am. John Donne has written that "No man is an island." He is correct. Even the Genesis writers knew that fact. "God created humankind in his image… male and female he created them." In fact, the Creator set humanity in families so the weak could be nurtured by the strong, and all would learn how to help each other move toward realizing their full potential. And because God has breathed life into all of us, we are all brothers and sisters. We are all colors. We are created with a variety of sexual preferences. We do not all look the same, and we possess different skills and interests. Across the years I have learned that there is much I do not know and understand. But that is all right.

ROLLING HILLS

I do know that sooner or later humanity will learn to accept one another as we are, or the struggle to make everyone conform to one understanding of life will destroy all humanity. So far as I am concerned, life is for living as we want, so long as we do not prevent others from fully living as well. I am still one who believes the Golden Rule should be the goal of all our behavior: "Do unto others as you would have others do unto you." I learned that rule in Sunday school when I was preschool age.

If we all lived toward achieving that positive relational focus in life, what a wonderful world could be established. Life is for living. And it is also for helping others live in such a way that they move toward their ultimate potential. So, relate to others and be supportive.

REFLECTIONS

Charles W. Hill, 1952

*My school picture,
1941-42*

*My wife, Betty L. Maze,
1952*

Barn on the Palmer Square farm. Taken 1928 by Uncle Ernest. This picture was mailed to Austin Hill who was working in Oklahoma.

House on the Palmer Square farm. Picture taken by Uncle Ernest on the same day as above photo. My family lived here from 1929 to 1945.

REFLECTIONS

*Bert Goddard Store, circa 1930,
Layman, Ohio, Washington County*

My dad "leading" a cow.

ROLLING HILLS

*Front: Bell and Charles Douglass, great-grandparents
Back left: Bessie Nutter Hill holding Charles Wayne
Back right: Grandmother Ella Douglass Nutter, 1935*

*Front Row: Grandmother Violet Hammer Simmons Hill; Austin Hill;
Bessie Nutter Hill; Ronnie Hill, son of Ernest; William (Bill) Hill.
Back Row: Florence Cain Hill, wife of Ernest Hill;
Charles Wayne Hill; Deloris Hill Kaneff; Lloyd Hill, 1948*

REFLECTIONS

The Beckner Cousins, left to right: Howard, Delbert, Uncle Tom, Aunt Helen, Paul, and Mary

This picture was taken in the 1940s at a family reunion. Left to right: Mary and Delbert Beckner; Richard "Dick" (front); Howard Beckner (behind Dick); I stand to the right.

Palmer Farm 1942, me, Richard, and Bill

Charles Hill, Austin (dad), William G. Hill, 1943

Richard Hill, Robert Warren, Ilene Henderson Hill, and Imogene Henderson, 1944

REFLECTIONS

Richard Lewis Hill, school photo, 1942-43

Richard in the new "duds" he purchased in June 1945.

Gravestone, Beverly, Ohio, Cemetery

Robert Warren Hill, school photo, 1938-39

Private Robert Warren Hill August 1944

Robert Warren Hill, 1944

REFLECTIONS

US Military Cemetery, Epinal, France
Private Robert Hill was buried here from November 1944-1947

Gravestone, Beverly, Ohio, Cemetery

Palmer Elementary School
Spring 1939*

Joyce and Jo Ann Porter,
James and John Pugh, 1940

*This picture was taken at Palmer Elementary School circa Spring of 1939, and was given to me many years ago by Mrs. Margaret Place who was, at the time of this photo, Miss Margaret Goddard, teacher of grades 1-4 at PES. The children are: Virginia Hill (unrelated to me), Howard Beckner (cousin), Paul Beckner (cousin), Ruth Pugh, Elma Pugh, Clara Knox (one of the Knox family mentioned in the book), Irene Hickman, Alice Reed, Ralph Hickman, Duane Porter, Fama Burt, Joel Gilliland, Joyce Porter (one of the twins mentioned in the book), Anna Wainwright, Junior Burchett, Eugene McIlvain (mentioned in the book), John Swain, Richard "Dick" Hill (my brother), Donald Trimble, Mary Ann Stollar, Paul Porter, Joan Porter (her twin is Joyce), Donna Jean Payne (mentioned in the book, later moved to the Bingham Farm), Mary Beckner (my cousin, note her bare feet), Kay Pugh (mentioned in the book), Harold Knox (brother to Clara, part of the Knox musicians). Miss Goddard is standing in back. Picture was taken at the north end front door where we entered every morning and exited each evening.

REFLECTIONS

Dion McDermott
Grades 5-8, 1940

Bonnie Brigham Ball, Music
Teacher; Margaret Goddard
Place, Grades 1-4, 1940

Vincent Basketball Team
1950-1951

County Champs
Sectional Runnerups

Coach:
Harvey W. Graham

Marvin Scott, 4; Ralph (Beanie) Barnett, g.; Don Roberts, g.;
Marvin Metheny, c.; Tom Barnett, 7; Lawrence Smith, Res.;
Carl Gaudy, Res.; Johnny Gaughan, Res.; Donald Greenless, Res.;
Denny Graham, 7; C. Wayne Hill, g.; Darrell Knosh, 7

ROLLING HILLS

This house is the place where I was born on 9-27-33, and where I lived until April 1945.

The farm where I was born.

House on the second farm where I lived from fall of 1946 until I married and left in 1953.

Barn in front of the second farm.

Vincent United Methodist Church

Palmer United Methodist Church

REFLECTIONS

I took this shot some years ago. The field of shocked corn is exactly how it would have looked when I was a kid.

www.ingramcontent.com/pod-product-compliance
Lightning Source LLC
LaVergne TN
LVHW041541070426
835507LV00011B/862